Pattern Sourcebook:
Japanese Style 2
250 Patterns for Projects and Designs

Shigeki Nakamura

BEVERLY MASSACHUSETTS

ROCKPORT PUBLISHERS

First published in the United States of America by
Rockport Publishers, a member of
Quayside Publishing Group
100 Cummings Center
Suite 406-L
Beverly, Massachusetts 01915-6101
Telephone: (978) 282-9590
Fax: (978) 283-2742
www.rockpub.com

ISBN-13: 978-1-59253-560-6
ISBN-10: 1-59253-560-7

10 9 8 7 6 5 4 3 2 1

Translation: Patricia Daly Oe (R.I.C. Publications)

Printed in Singapore

Preface

A long time ago I smiled when I spotted a sign in a small shop at an intersection in the Hongo district of Tokyo that said, "Our shop is just within the boundaries of the Edo district in Hongo."

When we hear the word "Edo," rather than the history of the "Edo era," we tend to see a series of images showing the proud character of the Edo people and the everyday lives of the ordinary citizens.

It is said that the 250-year-long peaceful Edo era represented a shift in the cultural focus from the samurai and upper classes to the townspeople and civilians. In particular, the activities of "the craftsmen" flourished in a free and broad-minded sense. There were all levels of craftsmen, but it was the characters of the "nuts-and-bolts" kind of artisan, the *Hatsuan* or *Kuma-san,* who always appear in the *Rakugo* stories, which really took center stage. At the heart of the Edo culture was the original character created by the concentration of the 300 domains (*han*) under the Shogunate of Greater Edo (Oedo).

This book focuses on the traditional patterns that strongly reflect the feel of "Edo." Materials that have depth, can easily be adapted, and are familiar have been carefully selected. Among them, the "Edo komon" (fine patterns of Edo) most appropriately represent the distinguishing features of the preferred style of the Edo craftsmen. These fine patterns reveal the elevated tastes of Edo, including stylishness, sophistication, smartness, and refinement. These qualities were not just confined to kimono patterns; they spread to all kinds of everyday items as well. This book aims to not duplicate any of the designs contained in the first book in the series, *Pattern Sourcebook: Japanese Style.*

We sincerely hope that the materials in this book can be used as a reference to further spread knowledge about exquisite Japanese traditional patterns.

Shigeki Nakamura (Cobble Collaboration)

Contents

How to Use This Book

Materials in the designs have been extracted from the existing traditional Edo patterns in order to focus on the main points specified in the text of this book. Our main goal is to present the patterns in a way that the structure of the design can be used for development. Consequently, we have modified many of the Edo-era traditional patterns and special features of the patterns to present them with our own original layout and coloring. Although the designs are based on the traditional designs, they are not the designs shown in their original form.

The files on the CD-ROM are, in principle, complete unit samples, but the images in the book have been trimmed to fit the layout, and the colors have been partially modified in some cases. Also, some of the files have been re-sized to fit the content of the CD-ROM.

Page Layout

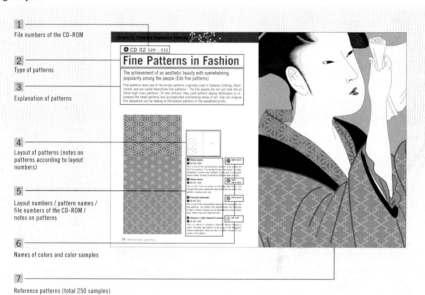

1 File numbers of the CD-ROM

2 Type of patterns

3 Explanation of patterns

4 Layout of patterns (notes on patterns according to layout numbers)

5 Layout numbers / pattern names / file numbers of the CD-ROM / notes on patterns

6 Names of colors and color samples

7 Reference patterns (total 250 samples)

Chapter 1
Everyday Patterns
CD 01:001-028

⊙ CD 01 001 – 004

Edo no Hana (Edo Style)

An abundance of designs. Original and dynamic patterns (Edo Style)

We associate "Edo Style" with "fire and fighting." We can understand the liveliness of the common people in the Edo era through this popular figure of speech. It was a dynamic era represented by the creativity of the different *matoi* (fireman's standard) designs of the "48 groups of firefighters." The lettering is used in the vaudeville storytelling scripts, Sumo, divine protection for the firefighters, and *ukiyoe* (woodblock-printing) designs. Such dynamic and original designs were created for future posterity.

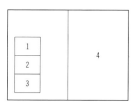

1 Mesh design
⊙ CD 01_001
This pattern has a wide range of applications from small emblems on kimono to material used in Noh costumes. It is also used as a paper lampshade at *Sensoji* temple.

deep orange

2 *Oirebukuro* (bags for bonuses)
⊙ CD 01_002
Recipients never know what was in these bags. Many variations of these designs have been produced since their origination in Edo times through to the present day.

3 *Matoi* (fireman's standard) pattern
⊙ CD 01_003
This is a unique design with randomly placed *matoi*, the standards used by the 48 groups of firefighters.

deep redange

4 *Matoi* and lettering
⊙ CD 01_004
This design is used for *Happi* cloth (coat), *Noren* (hanging cloth), tapestry, and so on. The *matoi* designs, used by all of the 48 groups of firefighters, convey a sense of manliness.

gray

Okamehyottoko **(fat-faced) mask** ●**CD 01_005** This is a good example of "symbolism" that can be applied uniquely or universally in a wide range of areas from religion to amusement.

dark green

***Hannya* (devil mask) pattern** ●CD 01_006 The ability of the Edo people to be daringly original is shown in the designs decorating the backs of clothing worn by clerics, which included this Hannya (devil mask), octopus, and crab patterns.

● plum color

⬤ CD 01 007 – 010
Kabuki

From the special to the everyday. Tasteful and sophisticated designs (Kabuki patterns)

Popular designer brands ould be considered the modern equivalent of the patterns created as a way for the Kabuki actors to assert themselves. The feature often inherent in those tasteful and sophisticated designs was their ability to separate from the individual *kabuki* actor and spread into the area of fashion. However, it is important to know the origin of these patterns.

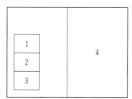

1 *Mimasumon* and *Kumadori* (Kabuki make-up)   ⬤ beige
⬤ CD 01_007

This is the family crest of the *Kabuki* Ichikawa family, but it became well-known as the large-patterned design on the sleeve of the kimono (*Suo*) worn by the Kabuki actor Hachidaime Ichikawa Danjuro.

2 *Mitsuoshima* (three broad stripes) pattern   ⬤ dark gray
⬤ CD 01_008

This is the family crest of the Bando Mitsugoro family. The combination of the large and light gourd design and the three broad stripes produces an exquisite effect. The refined taste in this design has made it popular for use in yukata (summer garment) and hand towels.

3 *Rokuyata* checked pattern   ⬤ dark green
⬤ CD 01_009

This pattern was used for the costumes of Okabe Rokuyata in kabuki performances and became known as the "Rokuyata check". Its usage spread as far as men's yukata. Its use has spread to men's yukata.

4 *Rokuyata* in kabuki
⬤ CD 01_010

This design was used in the woodblock prints of Utagawa Toyoko. Various patterns can be seen here, including the *sayakata* (grid) pattern, peony design, and cloud pattern.

⊙ CD 01 011 – 014

Actors' Patterns

Patterns in Kabuki and actors' clothing adapted for general appeal

Vaudeville theater was the greatest amusement for the Edo people. Whether it be in words or actions, whatever was expressed in the theater had an influence reaching right to the heart of the daily lives of the people. The main factor encouraging the surprisingly high uptake of trends was the visual element. This was even more so if it matched the tastes of the general public.

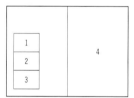

1 *Yokikotokiku* (Axe, koto, chrysanthemum)   ● **wine color**
⊙ CD 01_011

The pictorial puzzle of the axe (*yoki*), koto, and chrysanthemum (*kiku*) pattern can be read as "*Yokikotokiku*," which means "to hear good things." When expressions are created by using such fine patterns it is evident how easily these designs could become popular.

2 *Yokikotokiku* (Axe, koto, chrysanthemum) and *Kikugoro* checks
⊙ CD 01_012

You can see both the koto and the koto-pick in this design. The letters "ki" and "ro" are in the checked pattern formed by the four vertical lines and five horizontal lines. And in this way, the puzzle can be read as the name "Kikugoro."

3 Kamawanu - 1   ● **dark blue**
⊙ CD 01_013

This printed puzzle has been made by combining scythe (*kama*) with circle (*wa*) and the letter "nu." It is said to be an original idea by the Nanadaime Danjuro. The relaxed style of these prints can be seen elsewhere as well in many areas of people's everyday lives and language.

4 Kamawanu - 2   ● **dark blue**
⊙ CD 01_014

This sophisticated design soon became popular among the general public. It is a motif that is very appealing to use.

⦿ CD 01 015 – 018

Dance

Patterns incorporating actual elements of dancing

In any community, in any country, people derive great pleasure from watching dancers express the range of human emotions through the movement of their bodies. However, although special designs are often used for the dancers' costumes, it is rare to see examples of patterns that express elements of the actual dance itself.

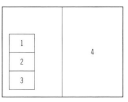

1 *Sanbanso*
⦿ CD 01_015

● plum color

Sanbanso means "The old man who is third to dance." It is a dance to pray for universal peace and a bumper harvest. The pattern incorporates decorative props from the dance (for example, the fans).

2 Connecting *Sanbanso*
⦿ CD 01_016

● fresh green
● mustard

This is an abstract adaptation of the pattern of small decorative props used in the *Sanbanso* dance pattern number 15. A unique striped design has been created.

3 *Shizuka Gozen*
⦿ CD 01_017

● dark violet

A delicate beauty is expressed through this arrangement of small decorative dance props and the petals of cherry blossoms.

4 *Kappore* design
⦿ CD 01_018

● Prussian blue

Kappore is a well-known Edo dance. In comparison to the liveliness of the songs and music, the costume designs have a relaxing *yukata*-quality to them and convey well the stylishness of the Edo people.

⊙ CD 01 019 – 022

Amusements

Patterns inspired by the level of enjoyment derived from amusements

Amusements enjoyed by people in Edo times do not differ greatly from those of the modern-day: theater, Sumo, learning and studying, *Igo* and *Shogi*. However, the level of enjoyment experienced through these activities appears to be deeper. This is shown by the fact that the props and toys used in amusements were made into fine patterns and these patterns themselves became fashionable.

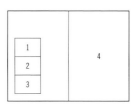

1 *Shamisen* pattern   ● purple
⊙ CD 01_019
The *shamisen* was always used for the songs that Edo people enjoyed and this pattern became popular among the general public.

2 Willow tree stripes and *Kemari*   ● grass green
⊙ CD 01_020
Along with cherry, pine, and maple, the willow tree was one of the trees used as a standard tree to measure the distance the ball was kicked in the ancient game of *Kemari*. These trees were planted on all four sides of the *Kemari* pitch.

3 *Shamisen* picks and *Koma* (Shogi pieces) pattern   ● brownish red
⊙ CD 01_021
Similar to pattern sample number 19, this is an interesting pattern that shows originality in its design.

4 *Yajirobei* pattern   ● Navy blue
⊙ CD 01_022
This pattern of balancing dolls is named after the character Yajirobei, who appeared in the book *Tokaidochuhizakurige*. Yajirobei balancing dolls were made to look as if he was carrying packages (by balancing them across his shoulders). His name was not only well-known as the balancing doll, but also as a collective term for the balancing games played in Edo times.

CD 01 023 – 026

Play

Qualities of "careful selection" and "subtlety" conveyed in patterns

In all areas of leisure enjoyed by the people of Edo, whether it be in *Ukiyoe*, *Gesaku* (popular novels), *Rakugo* or *Kokkeibon* (comic novels), their penchant to avoid the over-serious is evident. The ability of the people to appreciate a sense of humor suggests the maturity of the country. Also, the high cultural level of the people is demonstrated by their inclination towards careful selection and subtlety and this can be understood not only by their language, but also through the world of patterns.

1 *Narikin (the nouveau riche)*   ● brown
● CD 01_023

This design has an effective twist in the way the illustrated pattern on the *shogi* pieces is on the back rather than on the front. The development of this design coincided with the era that first identified the *nouveau riche*.

2 Arrangement of *Koma* (tops)   ● dark green
● CD 01_024

The tops are arranged in an orderly way, but the way the tops sometimes face in different directions is a good way to avoid making the pattern too fixed.

3 Dice spot pattern   ● Navy blue
● CD 01_025

Dice were used for fortune telling. However, the total number of spots on the two sides opposite each other always comes to seven, and there is no nine. The formation of the nine dots probably represents the square shape of the dice.

4 Edo Kites   ● brown
● CD 01_026

The kites in the Edo era were hand-painted   ● vermilion
Ukiyoe (woodblock prints). The "dragon" patterned kite is one famous kind of kite with a picture on it. That is a woodblock print. Another picture pattern is the "Waves and Rabbit," which depicts the waves and rabbit from the *Yokyoku* (Noh song) "*Chikubushima*." This design has been developed for family crests as well as for patterns.

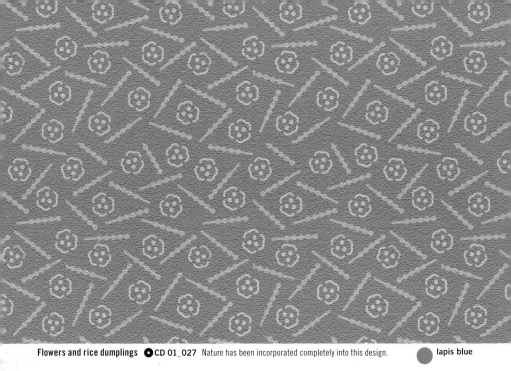

Flowers and rice dumplings ⬤CD 01_027 Nature has been incorporated completely into this design.

 lapis blue

Tying up monkeys ⬤CD 01_028 The tied-up monkey design represents the custom of using tied up cloth to represent the desire that customers do not leave. The movement conveyed by the curved lines shows originality.

auburn

Chapter 2
Plant and Vegetation Patterns
CD 02:029-088

CD 02 029 – 032

Fine Patterns in Fashion

The achievement of an aesthetic beauty with overwhelming popularity among the people (Edo fine patterns)

Fine patterns were one of the formal patterns originally used in Samurai clothing (*Kami-shimo*) and are called *Kamishimo* fine patterns." The Edo people did not just look idly at these high-class patterns. On the contrary, they used pattern-dyeing techniques to reproduce the small patterns and accomplished outstanding works of art. One can imagine this dynamism just by looking at the kimono patterns in the woodblock prints.

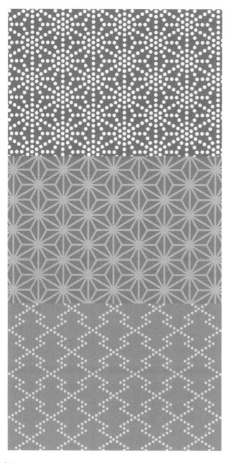

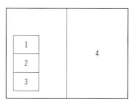

1 Hemp leaves · light plum
CD 02_029

This is one of the representative designs from among the Edo fine patterns. The wonderful way the design has been developed in diverse ways without it losing any of its original beauty shows the level of perfection that had been attained.

2 Hemp leaves · light lapis blue
CD 02_030

This is one of the variations on the hemp leaf theme. The straight lines give a pleasantly neat effect and are pretty. This pattern is popular even now.

3 Pine bark diamonds · olive green
CD 02_031

This is one of the representative designs from among the Edo fine patterns. The pattern also demonstrates the multitude of ways in which a design can be developed by using straight lines, dotted lines and composite lines.

4 Utamaro's *Bijin* (beautiful woman) · old rose
CD 02_032

This is a reprint of Utamaro's *Beautiful Woman Reading a Letter.* The hemp leaf pattern on the collar of the *Nagajuban* (kimono underwear), which are dots in pattern number 29, are circles in this pattern.

● CD 02 033 – 036

Elegance and Bad Taste

In Edo popular culture there is a saying: "Bright colors are in bad taste. Subdued colors are elegant."

Colors were regulated by the Shogunate, and bright colors were not allowed. However, brown and gray were permitted. The people outwitted the regulations by modifying these tones and developing "48 variations of brown and 100 variations of gray." These graceful and intelligent dyed colors, together with the profound sense conveyed by their names, formed the roots of this popular saying.

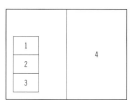

1 "Fallen plant life" stripes
● CD 02_033

 subdued blue

Rater than attractive blossoming flowers this pattern focuses its sympathy on plant life that has dropped to the ground. This pattern takes its name, "fallen plant life" from this concept and shows the subtlety of the Edo people's way of thinking.

2 Fallen pine leaves
● CD 02_034

pine leaf color

Modeled on the shape of the pine leaf, this design is a unique creation using free curved lines.

3 Fallen dried chrysanthemums
● CD 02_035

auburn

If you walk near someone wearing a kimono with this pattern you can probably almost smell the fragrance of chrysanthemums. This image that this work of art conveys suggests the painstaking care taken to produce it.

4 Variations on a striped flower theme
● CD 02_036

 subdued purple

This is a graceful striped design. The way the small flowers have been arranged in groups using the *kiribori* (dot drilling) technique produces an effect as if they have fallen or are drifting on a river.

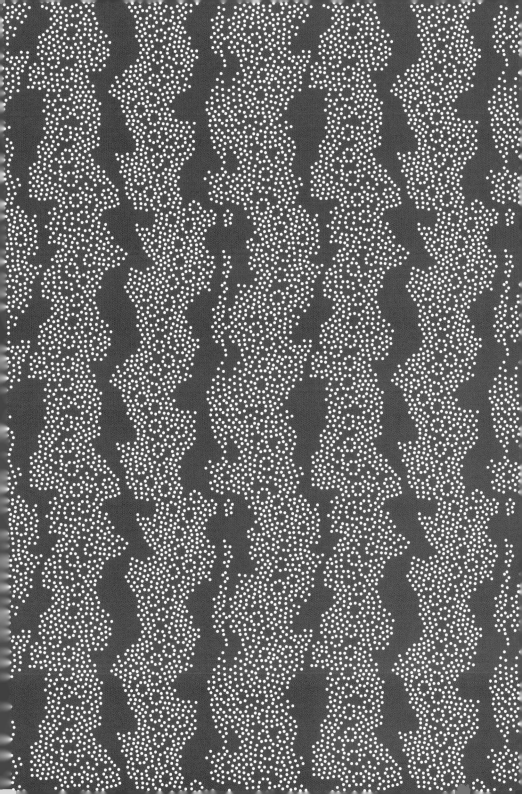

● CD 02 037 – 040

The Depth of Plain Color

The depth of plain color and the expanse of an endless image

Patterns drawn by *kiribori* alone and viewed from a distance appear like a solid color and convey the pride of the refined taste of people who wear those patterns. By only changing or adding one color, a completely different effect is produced. The attractiveness of the fine Edo patterns lies in their ability to create both depth in the plain, solid colors and the expanse of an endless image.

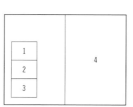

1 Ginkgo leaves and tied letters ● old rose
● CD 02_037
This pattern is used in many different ways so the color tones are not fixed.

2 Gourd pattern ● light blue
● CD 02_038
Although this pattern is simple it shows an exquisite taste. The unique shapes and layout of the pattern are effective.

3 Hagi (Japanese bush clover) ● light green
● CD 02_039
When bush clover is used this way in fine patterns, the image of autumn, as found in *Yuzen* works, is down-played.

4 Dandelion clocks ● dandelion
● CD 02_040
This fine pattern is a lovely and realistic representation. It inspires a desire to try out the effects of changing the color.

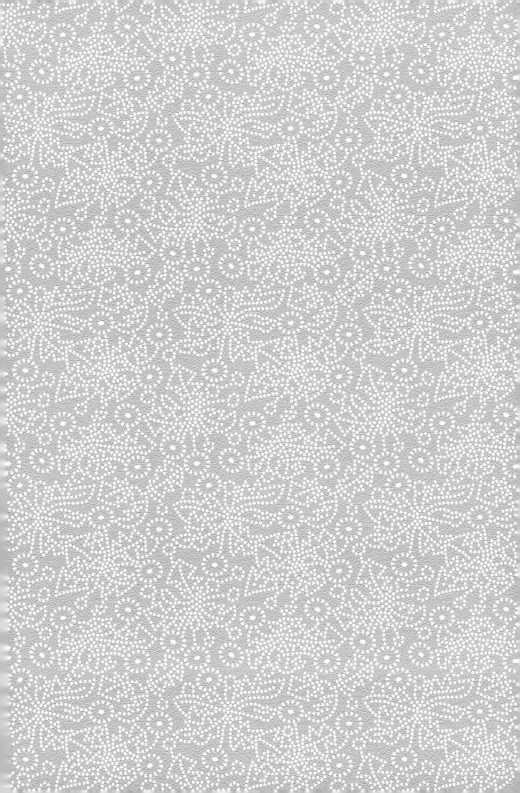

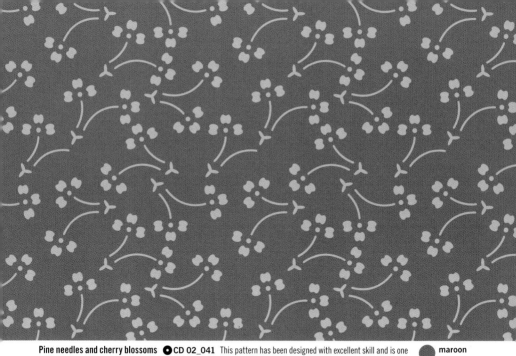

Pine needles and cherry blossoms ●CD 02_041 This pattern has been designed with excellent skill and is one of the top fine patterns. It shows originality, and as a woven pattern, the hidden beauty of the design is brought out.

 maroon

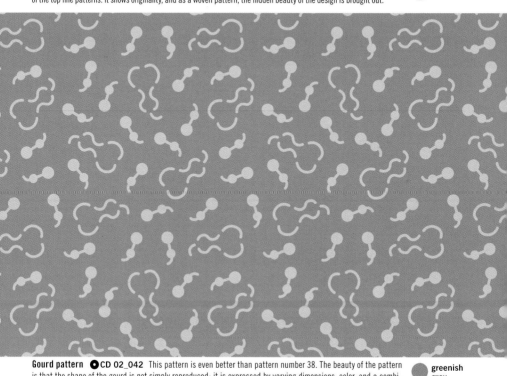

Gourd pattern ●CD 02_042 This pattern is even better than pattern number 38. The beauty of the pattern is that the shape of the gourd is not simply reproduced; it is expressed by varying dimensions, color, and a combination of different lines.

greenish gray

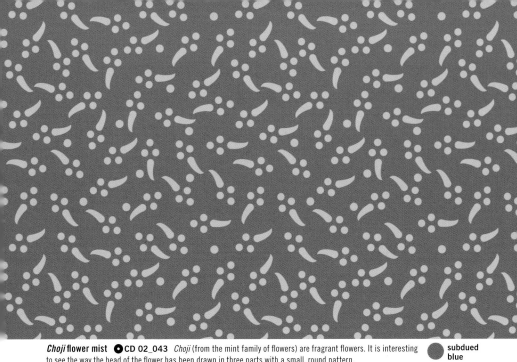

Choji **flower mist** ⏺CD 02_043 *Choji* (from the mint family of flowers) are fragrant flowers. It is interesting to see the way the head of the flower has been drawn in three parts with a small, round pattern.

subdued blue

Nanten (**sacred bamboo**) ⏺CD 02_044 This is a realistic portrayal of sacred bamboo.

auburn

● CD 02 045 – 048
Design Skill

Edo era patterns created by an elevated sensitivity

People in the Edo era seem to have been highly sensitive. We could almost go as far as to say that their sensitivity toward nature was second to none. Proof of this skill can be seen in the way that designs that express nature have been passed down through the generations and are now classical archetypes.

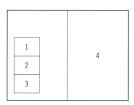

1 Fine plum blossom pattern ● dark lilac
● CD 02_045
There are innumerable excellent plum patterns. This one goes beyond reality to express even the fragrance of plum blossoms in its symbolic design.

2 Scattered plum blossoms and diamond bars ● lapis blue
● CD 02_046
This is not just a plum blossom pattern. By the simple addition of diamond shapes in bars it demonstrates the excellent way that the depth of a three-dimensional effect can be achieved.

3 Plum blossoms and *Mino* (straw raincoat) ● plum color
● CD 02_047 ● smoke gray
This gives the impression of plum blossoms being splashed by rain. The *Mino* raincoats are strung together in a vine creating an endless and interesting fine pattern. Although it incorporates two motifs the design is not confusing.

4 Cherry blossom pattern on a decorative comb ● dark green
● CD 02_048
By incorporating a cherry blossom pattern inlay various kinds of small objects can be made even more beautiful. This pattern creates a high-class effect by the precision skills with which the pattern is produced in a moderate way.

○ CD 02 049 – 052

Design Development Skills

Examples of the excellent skills of the Edo artisans to transform the same motif in a myriad ways

In the following patterns, we can see the fine skills of the Edo craftsmen in their ability to express the same motif in many different ways. These excellent skills were also developed as a result of the elevated sensitivity toward beauty possessed by the Edo people. These patterns convey the special ability of the Edo people to create a type of beauty that respected modesty.

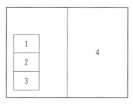

1 Badger and Chrysanthemum
○ CD 02_049

 light scarlet

The intricate detail of the chrysanthemum petals produces an effect resembling the fur of a badger. It is a wonderful fine pattern that infuses the petals with vitality.

2 Diamond Chrysanthemums
○ CD 02_050

dark violet

There are many fine patterns that re-shape the chrysanthemum into a diamond shape. This is an excellent work of art showing the potential for design development inherent in the pattern.

3 Circular chrysanthemum vine arabesque pattern
○ CD 02_051

green-blue

A medium-sized pattern. This is an original expression combining an abstract chrysanthemum pattern with a concrete representation of a vine.

4 Chrysanthemum arabesque design
○ CD 02_052

indigo

This is a pattern-dyed print. During the Edo period, techniques were developed and perfected to produce arabic patterns and dyeing along with the creation of original Japanese colors.

Pine, bamboo and plum pattern ● CD 02_053 An exquisite and rarely seen work of art. The plum blossoms and pine needles are contained within the frames made by the sticks of bamboo.

dusky pink

Floral checked pattern ● CD 02_054 This looks like a lively checked pattern but when viewed from a distance it enhances the depth of the color.

light steel blue

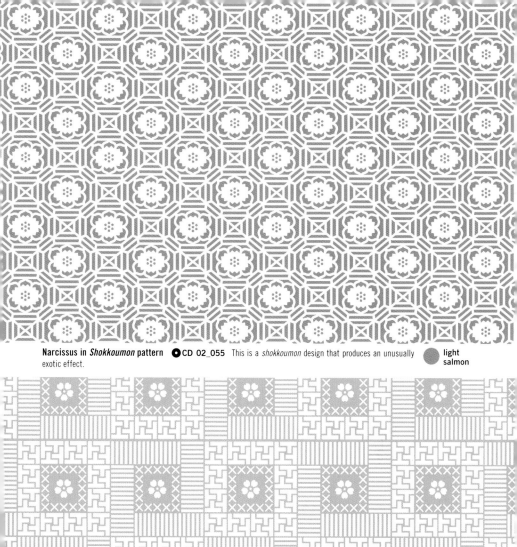

Narcissus in *Shokkoumon* pattern ●CD 02_055 This is a *shokkoumon* design that produces an unusually exotic effect.

● light salmon

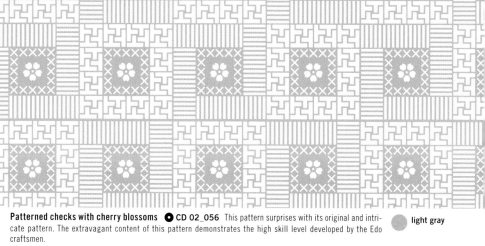

Patterned checks with cherry blossoms ● CD 02_056 This pattern surprises with its original and intricate pattern. The extravagant content of this pattern demonstrates the high skill level developed by the Edo craftsmen.

● light gray

◉ CD 02 057 – 060

Playfulness

Success of Edo fine patterns developed from friendly competition between the experts in paper pattern engraving and those in dyeing

Both the skills of engraving and dyeing that were used to create fine patterns in the Edo era required a high level of technical expertise. Craftsmen competed with each other to produce the most detailed patterns. However, they did not only compete in the area of technical skill, they were also continuously challenging themselves to create new and interesting ideas for designs. Fine Edo patterns fully flourished as a result of this friendly competition.

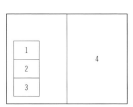

1 Bamboo stripes 　　　　　●dark verdant green
◉CD 02_057

Bamboo is named as one of the "four gentlemen" in Japanese traditional art along with the orchid, chrysanthemum and plum. For that reason it is often seen in fine Edo patterns.

2 Plovers in bamboo 　　　　　●dark blue
◉CD 02_058

As the use of color was limited, it was difficult to express the feel of the four seasons properly. However, when color tones are used in a certain way, as in this example, the atmosphere of the four seasons can be felt.

3 Orchids 　　　　　●purple
◉CD 02_059

When arranging the random layout of a pattern, there is no end to concerns about balance. But at these times we can refer to and learn from the artistic sense of our ancestors.

4 Dancing paulownia 　　　　　●dark olive green
◉CD 02_060

Free and open-minded expressions show the sense of playfulness of the Edo artisans. All four of the examples on this page convey this idea.

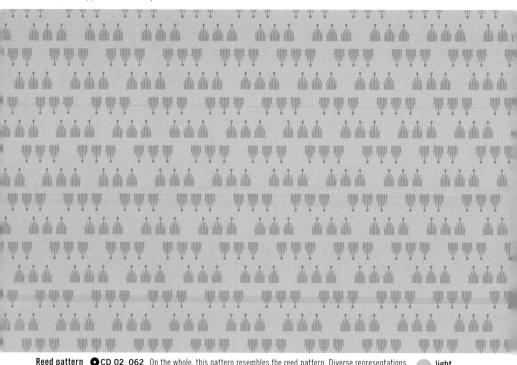

Reed leather pattern ●CD 02_061 A pattern of reeds found at the riverside. The meaning of the leather is
unclear, but it appears to be a reed pattern branded into leather.   **silver gray**

Reed pattern ●CD 02_062 On the whole, this pattern resembles the reed pattern. Diverse representations
of water scenes can be expressed by varying the layout.

**light
green**

Reeds on water pattern ●CD 02_063 The water is sparkling with the reflection of sunlight. It is a relaxing pattern that certainly conveys the movement of the water in the realistic scene.

light blue

Pattern of irises and small flowers ●CD 02_064 This is a typical design, but it can be modified in many ways by different combinations of motifs.

 lilac

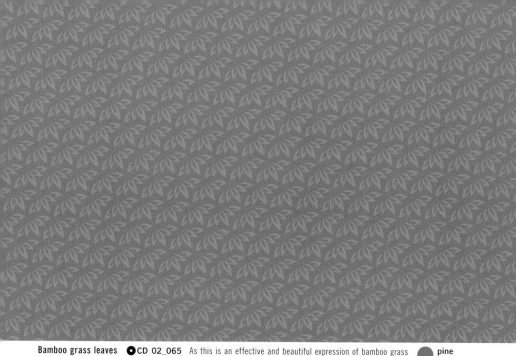

Bamboo grass leaves ●CD 02_065 As this is an effective and beautiful expression of bamboo grass leaves, it makes a very attractive fine pattern even though it has a routine layout.

pine green

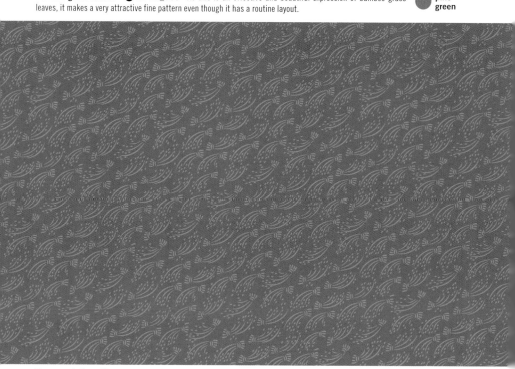

Sheaves of rice ●CD 02_066 Although this is a systematic, rather than a random, arrangement of the motif, it creates an interesting diagonal-line effect.

 brown

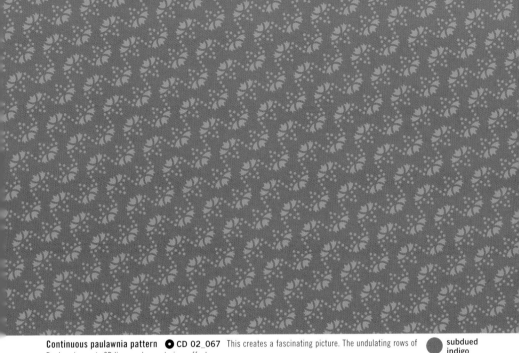

Continuous paulawnia pattern ⬤ CD 02_067 This creates a fascinating picture. The undulating rows of Paulawnia create 3D lines and a mysterious effect.

 subdued indigo

Pine and wisteria ⬤ CD 02_068 This is an example of how one solid color can be used for a fine design to create an effective impression.

 Edo purple

Peony flowers in changing stripes ● CD 02_069 This is the middle of the pattern. The impression the pattern gives varies greatly according to the colors used. This design will probably be either loved or hated.

deep crimson

***Miru* (sea staghorn) pattern**   ●CD 02_070   Sea staghorn is a kind of seaweed that clings to rocks and stones in shallow sea water. Edo taste is shown more in the bold contrast between the two circular patterns rather than in the portrayal of the staghorn itself. It is difficult to modify the color in this design.

sea staghorn color

● CD 02 071 – 074

Abstract Patterns

Artisans' skills created unlimited abstract patterns.

In order to start to dye a fine pattern and place glue on the appropriate parts, the pattern is cut out from the paper with a pattern stencil. In order to cut around these precise patterns various tools, including knives, are used. For example, by the use of *Kiribori*, *Tsukibori*, and *Yumibori* tools, dots or circles can be drilled by rotating the semi-circular blade. The artisans who were experts at their craft make it look so simple to create these abstract floral patterns, and there are an infinite number of variations.

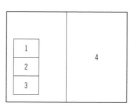

1 Flower and leaf check   ● mint green
● CD 02_071

This is an expression of a ground color that is often seen. The effect of the pattern can be altered in an endless number of ways by changing the repetition, combination, or arrangement of the same pattern.

2 Flowers and mist   ● rose red
● CD 02_072

There are no other patterns that are so undeniably an expression of the formlessness of "mist."

3 Small flowers   ● wisteria
● CD 02_073

There are many different small-flower patterns. Even a small modification can lead to a big change in design.

4 Variation on a flower theme   ● cyan
● CD 02_074

This is an elegant pattern. Snow can also be expressed in this pattern depending on the coloring.

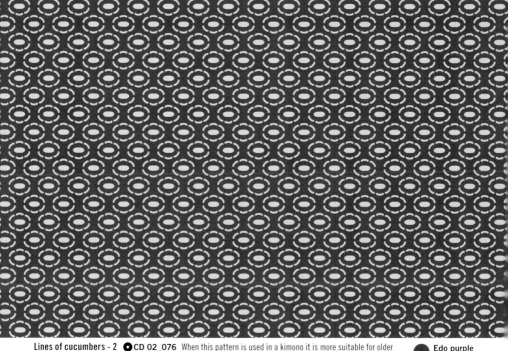

Lines of cucumbers - 1 ●CD 02_075 This pattern could be seen either as a cucumber or as a Japanese quince flower pattern.

 pine color

Lines of cucumbers - 2 ●CD 02_076 When this pattern is used in a kimono it is more suitable for older people, compared to the same motif used in the pattern number 75.

● Edo purple

Clover *unsai* ⊙ CD 02_077 *Unsai* can mean either "cloud colors" or "cloud edges." This pattern is an expression of the sky whichever meaning is used.

● crimson

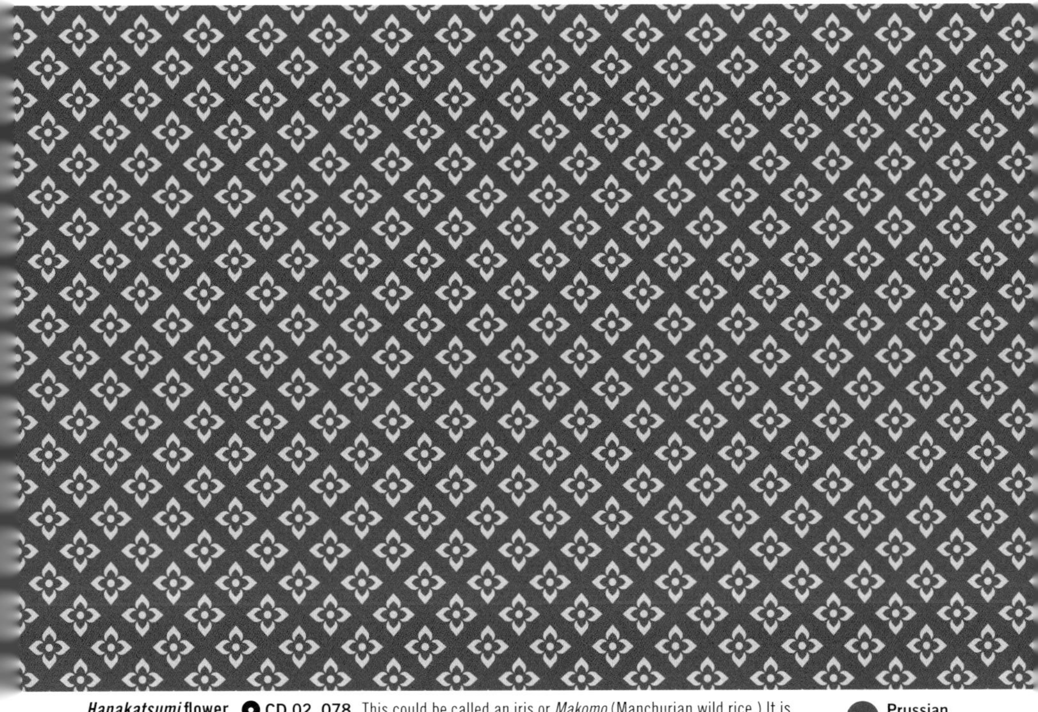

Hanakatsumi flower ⊙ CD 02_078 This could be called an iris or *Makomo* (Manchurian wild rice.) It is unclear which is correct. In any case, this pattern has been used for singing since a long time ago.

● Prussian blue

Lines of flowers ⬤ **CD 02_079** This was a fine pattern developed using the *Kiribori* technique. It shows a special skill in the way the four corners of the oval shapes containing the flowers form cotton reel shapes.

cherry blossom color

Floral Checks ⬤**CD 02_080** It is important how the flowers (the subject of the pattern) are arranged so that they stand out from the checks.

 light fawn

Floral diagonal checks ●CD 02_081   There is a free sense to this diagonal check. When looked at directly
it creates yet another effect.

light blue

Lines of Chinese flowers ●CD 02_082   Most of the Chinese flowers in Edo patterns take this shape.
Because the pattern was modeled on a foreign flower, it is unlikely to represent the Japanese wild *Karahanaso*.

**creamy
green**

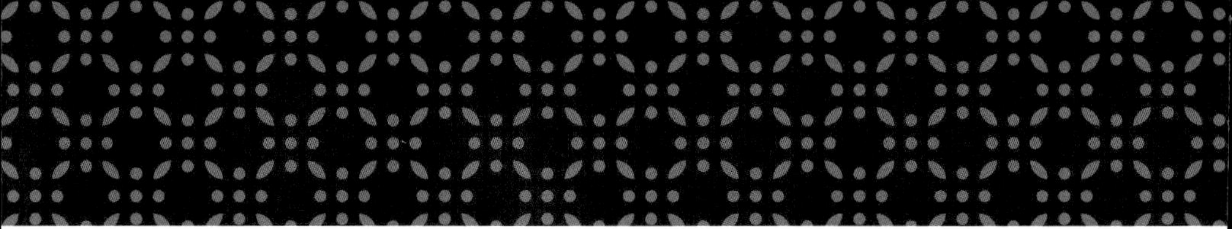

Petals ●CD 02_083   This pattern shows the mysterious qualities of the fine patterns; they are both beautiful and precise and are painstakingly made.

● dark indigo

Four diamonds and petals ●CD 02_084   Although the "four diamond" pattern is also called "*Takeda* diamond," it appears to be used here without any connection to that name.

● dark maroon

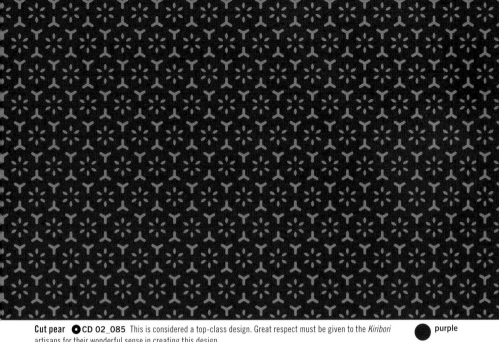

Cut pear ●CD 02_085 This is considered a top-class design. Great respect must be given to the *Kiribori* artisans for their wonderful sense in creating this design.

 purple

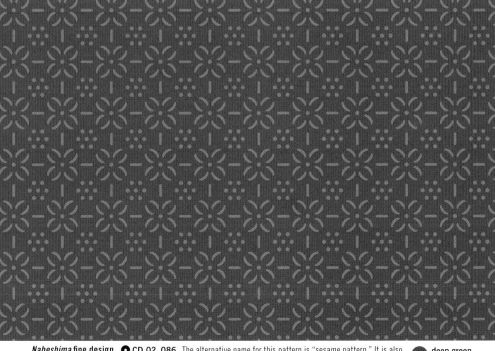

***Nabeshima* fine design** ● CD 02_086 The alternative name for this pattern is "sesame pattern." It is also famous in Kagahan Maeda's "chrysanthemum diamonds" and Satsumahan Shimizu's "small and large *arare*."

 deep green

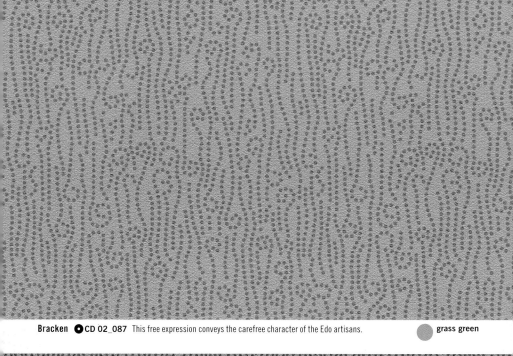

Bracken ●CD 02_087 This free expression conveys the carefree character of the Edo artisans.

grass green

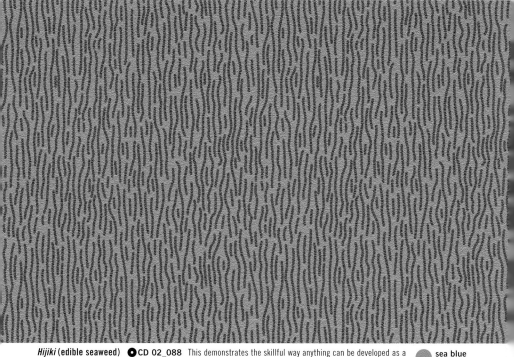

Hijiki (edible seaweed) ●CD 02_088 This demonstrates the skillful way anything can be developed as a fine pattern. This pattern is unique.

 sea blue

Chapter 3
Animal Patterns
CD 03:089-104

⊙ CD 03 089 – 092
Symbolism

The precision of symbolism can be seen in these traditional patterns.

Things are turned into symbols, given a shape, acknowledged and become established. We draw great benefits from the hard work of our ancestors. It is easy to just say "that's tradition," but from now can we meet the challenge of continuing to create wonderful new designs conveying universal patterns with precision?

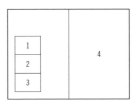

1 Folded cranes
⊙ CD 03_089
         ● purple

The folded crane design represents both a symbolic and concrete pattern. "The folded crane" is a widely recognized, extremely well-known shape.

2 Lion pattern
⊙ CD 03_090
         ● bright green

This design represents the lion. Not simply because it has been used for such a long time, but also because the shape is actually recognized as "lion fur."

3 Lion fur in *Gunome* (irregular semi-circles)
⊙ CD 03_091
         ● reddish orange

The name of this pattern and its layout (*Gunome*) are well known. It is a little different to the patterns used for plant life.

4 Lion kimono for dancing
⊙ CD 03_092
         ● dark green

This is an example of a lion pattern in actual use on a *Hakama*. The cloth is raised on the outside without breaking up the lion pattern.

⦿ CD 03 093 – 096

Lightheartedness

Small animal patterns combining light-hearted and auspicious images

Most of the animals appearing in the fine patterns are small animals that have an auspicious image such as birds, insects, small fish and bats. Dragonflies and butterflies are particularly common, as well. The reason being that these small life-forms have a light-hearted feel to them. In contrast to plant patterns these designs appeal to people who associate them with the image of lively young town girls.

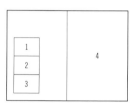

1 Water birds   ● sky blue
⦿ CD 03_093
This fine pattern is appropriate for summer. The plover pattern is drawn with waves, and this pattern could be enhanced by incorporating a clear background of flowing water.

2 Sparrow pattern   ● willow green
⦿ CD 03_094
A familiar bird is used in this realistic pattern and a skillful and attractive effect has been created.

3 Firefly squid pattern   ● light steel blue
⦿ CD 03_095
This is an unusual spring motif, appealing to the seasonal aesthetic tastes of the Edo people.

4 Dragonfly pattern   ● dark orange
⦿ CD 03_096
This motif is often seen on Samurai armor, but when used as a fine pattern it creates a pretty and elegant effect.

CD 03 097 – 100

Prayers

Motifs carefully chosen for their "wishful" and "good-fortune" qualities

Although plant motifs do not have any particular associations with good fortune, the opposite is true of animal motifs. The subjects selected for fine patterns are small and familiar animals, birds and insects, but they are not always necessarily symbols of good-fortune.

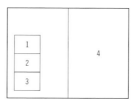

1	4
2	
3	

1 *Karigane* (White-fronted Goose) ties cobalt blue
● CD 03_097

The *Karigane* goose is said to bring good fortune.

2 Continuous pattern of bats ● brown
● CD 03_098

This is a well-known, auspicious pattern. It produces the same kind of effect as one in pattern number 67, the continuous *Paulawnia* pattern.

3 Diamonds of cranes facing opposite directions ● mid-purple
● CD 03_099

This is an auspicious pattern. The negative pattern of the cranes and their arrangement within the diamond shapes create the illusory effect of the cranes seeming to disappear.

4 *Tokusa* (scouring rush) and cranes facing opposite directions ● dark green
● CD 03_100

This is a famous fine pattern that signified nobility and high class culture.

Butterflies on bamboo stripes ●CD 03_101 The great pattern masters recognized the spiritual qualities of rebirth and reincarnation in the butterfly image, and most of the butterfly patterns give this impression.

light
bamboo

Small wading birds in checked pattern ●CD 03_102 Small birds and clouds can be seen inside each check. The way that the birds and clouds are brought to life strongly conveys the vitality of the artisans.

 lilac

***Manekineko* (welcoming cat) pattern**   ●CD 03_103   The *Manekineko* is just as popular nowadays as it was in Edo times. Used as a good luck charm for starting new businesses, it is said to bring prosperity.

● cherry
red

***Inuhariko* (papier-mache dog pattern)**   ●CD 03_104   The shape of the Chinese character for "laugh" is incorporated into this pattern in a humorous way. This pattern conveys the relaxed feel of the Edo people.

 blue

Chapter 4
Utensil Patterns
CD 04:105-146

● CD 04 105 – 108

The Edo Atmosphere

Patterns of the Edo atmosphere created by the pride of the Edo people

There is a saying, "Edo manners." Old Edo was very crowded; over half of the space in the city was used for the shogun's housing and in the remaining space the people had to live closely together—and in harmony. The foundation for this harmony was built on the social manners that the Edo people learned and taught with pride. The Edo atmosphere was created and strengthened by this consciousness.

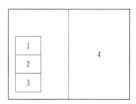

1 *Shifuku* (a silk pouch used in the tea ceremony)
● CD 04_105

persimmon orange

This pattern share's its name with a pouch used in a tea ceremony.

2 *Chadoguzukushi* (whisk used in the tea ceremony)
● CD 04_106

green tea color

This aesthetic implement does not lose any of its beauty in this fine pattern.

3 Scattered *Noshi* (auspicious symbol attached to the wrapping of a gift)
● CD 04_107

purple

This symbol has been used for a long time as a congratulatory decoration applied as a wrapping attachment for formal occasions. It means "eternal continuation." Originally, a *Noshi* was a dried strip of abalone wrapped in paper folded in a hexagonal way.

4 Unrestrained pattern of *Noshi*
● CD 04_108

This is an excellent expression of a *Noshi* pattern. The motif is conveyed in an unrestrained, natural way showing a blend of different designs flying up at the ends. Like the *baren* weave, this pattern has a good reputation and represents the resilient nature of the Edo people.

⦿ CD 04 109 – 112

Suehiro Folding Fans

Folding fans used as a motif for fine patterns

These patterns take their names from the shape of the motif, which is an unfolded fan. There are a great many patterns incorporating the fan motif, of course, including fine patterns. This is not only because it has a beautiful shape, but also because it was customarily used in everyday life.

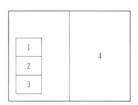

1 Stripes of connecting fans
⦿ CD 04_109
fresh green

With its neatly arranged lines of fans, this pattern gives off a comfortable impression. Also, an interesting 3D effect has been achieved thanks to the way the fans are lined up against each other.

2 Bird *Tasuki* (a band of cloth used for holding kimono sleeves out of the way) on fan
⦿ CD 04_110
nightingale brown

This continuous pattern was used in connection with the cloisonné design. It is a tasteful *Tasuki* design, incorporating wavy lines of fans that form stripes.

3 Connecting fans on reins
⦿ CD 04_111
plum color

The artisan who created this pattern must have been able to clearly see fans in the design, but viewers may need a little more clarity.

4 Lines of fans
⦿ CD 04_112
sapphire blue

Each fan unit is so pretty that this design has more of a pleasant charm than elegance to it.

Fan pattern ●CD 04_113 This elegant design invites you to change the color tone and pattern of the fans.

 gentian

Peony and fan pattern ●CD 04_114   This pattern is so good that it almost looks like this fine pattern has been modeled on a *Yuzen* pattern and a reproduction of a famous work of art by woodblock print.

 light green

● CD 04 115 – 118

Seasonal Festivals

Patterns developed through the custom of performing ceremonies

Celebrations for the Chrysanthemum Festival were taken far more seriously in the past, compared to now. Fixed ceremonies were not only celebrated by the samurai class, but also by the Edo people, who incorporated them into their daily lives in a lively fashion.

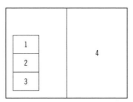

1 **Dolls**   light pink
● CD 04_115

Even if you look at this pattern up closely it is hard to make out what the design is. If you look at it from a distance and the dotted lines appear joined up it is still a puzzle what the figures actually are.

2 **Doll developments**   old yellow
● CD 04_116

In this pretty pattern, although there are not many lines, it is possible to distinguish that the figures are dolls at a glance.

3 **Stripes of paper-dolls**   white-green
● CD 04_117

This is an abstract pattern. However, if this pattern was on the kimono of a girl standing in front of a *Hinadan* (tiered display of dolls for Girls's Day) it could be viewed as a representation of the *Hinadan* itself.

4 **Scattered standing paper doll pattern**   deep red
● CD 04_118

The pattern of paper dolls on an autumn-flower background pattern is one that is often seen. There may be a little confusion now, though, because a long time ago the doll festival was also held in August and September.

● CD 04 119 – 122

Trade

Discover a realm of patterns that reflect the activities of the Edo tradesmen.

Edo was a city of consumers. From a Western perspective it could be described as a thriving capitalist economic system. Many words and themes connected with money originated in the Edo era. The activities of tradesmen, both good and bad, often appear in plays from this period. Their activities are also reflected in the following patterns, however, note that the cashiers in the shops did not go as far as wearing kimonos with the trading weights pattern.

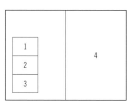

1 Three-bar weight pattern
● CD 04_119
● dark green

Weights used for trading, which was a symbol often used in patterns seen in family crests, nowadays is often used as a company symbol.

2 *Tawara* (straw bag) for rice
● CD 04_120
● brown

The *Tawara* (straw bags) were always the same, featuring rounded corners and high-class fine patterns, whether they were used for rice or charcoal.

3 *Soroban* (abacus) stripes
● CD 04_121
● grayish purple

You may recognize this as an abacus pattern. When used in a kimono pattern, it would usually be on those worn by the children of merchant families or workers.

4 Climbing ivy weights
● CD 04_122
● dark clay green
● dark iron blue

Although this uses the same trading weights pattern, it is more of a high-class pattern.
Ivy is a robust plant that represents fertility and a flourishing business. This is a typical design of ivy and weights.

Fern and *Takarazukushi* (treasures) pattern ●CD 04_123 The equivalent of the modern popular lottery
Takarakuji was called *Tomikuji* in the Edo era, and it was the dream of the Edo citizens to win.

 light
orange

Takarazukushi (treasures) ●CD 04_124 This pattern appears to have been made with the desire to own treasures even if only in the designs of fine patterns. Although the motifs themselves may be rather low-class, the dot drilling technique used to make the design gives it a high-class effect.

deep
orange

⊙ CD 04 125 – 128
Everyday Objects

Edo fine patterns elevate the beauty of everyday items.

Just like in modern times, people in the Edo era had many objects in their daily lives yet they still wanted more. One can imagine that the lives of the Edo people, nonetheless, were full of warmth. And one can understand the affection felt toward things and the warmth of the expressions used in language by looking at their fine patterns and hearing the names they gave those patterns.

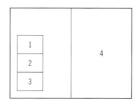

1 *Daruma*　　　　　　　　　　　● pink
⊙ CD 04_125

The small *Daruma* doll shapes in the process of sitting up give this pattern a humorous touch.

2 Lines of cotton reels　　　　　　● grey-green
⊙ CD 04_126

The cotton reel shape is modified in many different ways for patterns. The fact that this motif is used in family crests even today is evidence of how such a small, everyday object could be held in reverence.

3 Vase pattern　　　　　　　　　　● brown
⊙ CD 04_127

This is an arrangement of small vases. Because the shapes overlap, the pattern may appear more like acorns. One can imagine that this was a vase much-loved by the artisan.

4 Lines of paintbrushes　　　　　　● lilac
⊙ CD 04_128

The effect created by the contrast between the solid paint-brush pattern and the brushed hairs is fascinating. A tasteful diamond pattern is produced by the outstanding curved lines.

● CD 04 129 – 132

Basket-weave

Basket-weave pattern that became popular due to their power to ward off evil

There was a belief that the basket-weave pattern could ward off evil. The idea was that if the devil was trying to get into a house he would be so busy counting the dangling basket-weave pattern that the night would end before he could enter. Even though there is a strong magnetism to this pattern—just as the superstition suggests— even more, it conveys the affectionate sense of the Edo people, who always wanted the best for people.

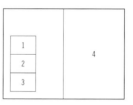

1 Basket-weave ● brown
● CD 04_129

Although, this basket-weave pattern, created by the *Kiribori* dot-drilling technique, looks simple, it displays a special design skill.

2 Basket-weave pattern - 1 ● mustard
● CD 04_130

This is an established basket-weave pattern. It is a geometric pattern with a religious beauty.

3 Basket-weave pattern - 2 ● brown
● CD 04_131

This pattern incorporates two sticks of bamboo, which represent a strong will.

4 Large basket-weave pattern ● grayish brown
● CD 04_132

This is a simple pattern that possesses a beautiful and refined balance. Because it does not have any overbearing qualities to it, this pattern is often used for fabric.

● CD 04 133 – 136

Talent

Displays of the expertise of the Edo artisans had in dyeing and reproducing intricately hand-woven patterns.

Fine patterns are dyed. It may be difficult to reproduce in a dyed pattern the same depth of quality attained in a pattern that is hand-woven with thread. But one aspect of the resourcefulness of the Edo artisans lay in their ability to take the motif from a woven pattern and, with their expertise, change the name of the design into proper nouns. The woven patterns *Igeta* and *Yagasuri* in the following pages are examples of this.

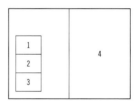

1 Splashed *Igeta* pattern ● light blue
● CD 04_133
This is a design woven in cotton. However, the nature of the design differs according to rural or urban use.

2 Plovers on *Igeta* pattern ● ultramarine blue
● CD 04_134
This design shows the special ability of the Edo artisans. By adding the plovers to the *Igeta* design a different effect is produced.

3 Variation of an *Igeta* pattern ● turquoise
● CD 04_135
This pattern takes on a completely different shape in this elegant *Igeta* design.

4 *Igeta* checked variation ● dark green
● CD 04_136
One can almost hear an Edo citizen saying, "Hey, don't you think it's impossible to weave such an amazing pattern?" This pattern displays a definite transformation into a complex, detailed pattern.

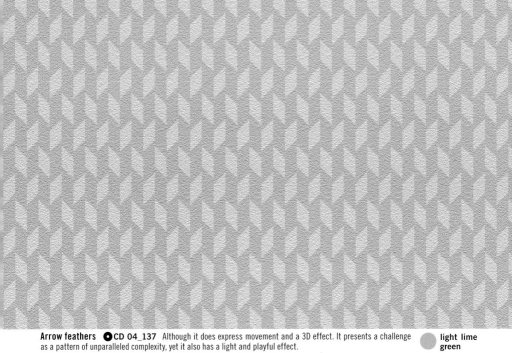

Arrow feathers ●CD 04_137 Although it does express movement and a 3D effect. It presents a challenge as a pattern of unparalleled complexity, yet it also has a light and playful effect.

light lime green

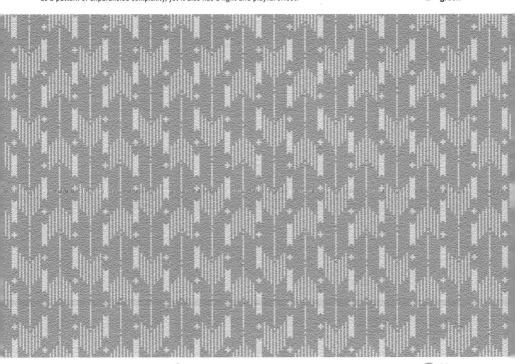

Stripes of modified arrow feathers ●CD 04_138 A natural looking fine pattern of arrows.

blue

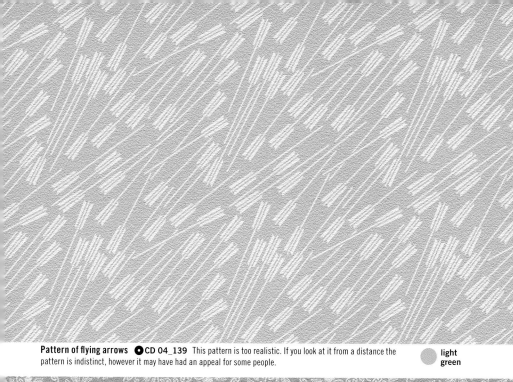

Pattern of flying arrows ●CD 04_139 This pattern is too realistic. If you look at it from a distance the pattern is indistinct, however it may have had an appeal for some people.

light green

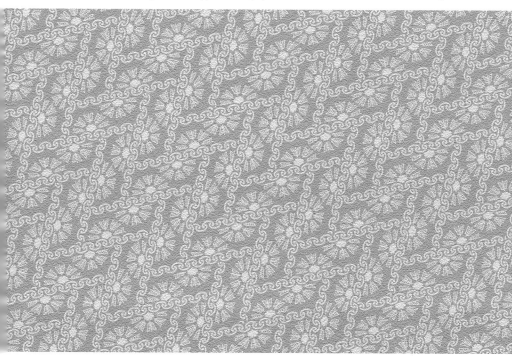

Arrow wheel pattern ●CD 04_140 A beautiful effect can be achieved by endlessly connecting small pattern units. But in this case, it's almost as if the pattern needs to be tidied up a little more.

blue

● CD 04 141 – 144

Material for Development

Patterns from which one may learn and develop designs.

Motifs are randomly chosen from among everyday objects and developed into fine patterns. We can only stand back and admire the skill it took to take an everyday object, make it into a motif for a fine pattern, and transform it into a beautiful design. However, we can't help but wonder what the reaction of people was when seeing unusual objects that they rarely come into contact with used in kimono patterns. Were they shocked? Did they reject such patterns? The fact remains that we can learn a lot from this skillful selection of motifs and way the designs were arranged.

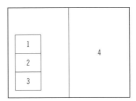

1 Roof
● CD 04_141

dark green

This is a rather ordinary pattern. Refer to pattern number 53, in which a pine, plum, and bamboo design is inserted into the squares.

2 Scattered traps
● CD 04_142

dark brown

This probably represents rabbit traps—a rather surprising choice as a motif.

3 Horse-bit connecting pattern
● CD 04_143

dark green

Horse bits are also used as family crests, but the metal part of the bit is taken off in the emblem of the Shimazu family, for instance. Note, however, the way the cushions connect the horse bits in this pattern shows a special design skill.

4 Zigzag pattern
● CD 04_144

dark green and brown

This zigzag pattern represents the steps on a pier that enabled luggage to be lowered even when it is high tide. It is a rather dignified pattern.

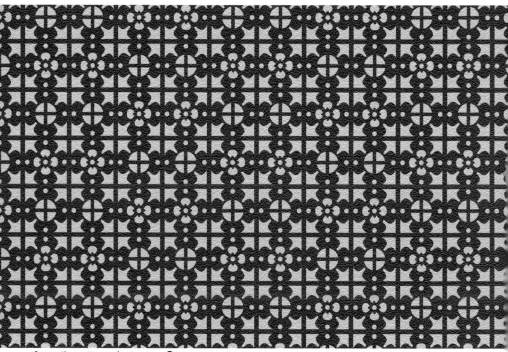

Drawer handles and fittings ⬤CD 04_145 *Kan* are the visible metal fittings used to open drawers. Because the shape of one unit is interesting, can be developed in many different, yet fulfilling, ways.

⬤ subdued orange

Connecting patterns of cut paper ⬤CD 04_146 Everyone has, folded a piece of paper, made cuts, and opened it up to form patterned paper. This is such a connecting pattern.

 violet

Chapter 5
Patterns from Nature
CD 05:147-176

● CD 05 147 – 150

Inase (Dashing style)

Words cherished by Edo people such as *Inase* (dashing style) and *Iki* (fashionable)

Just as the name Edo suggests (the "E" means "estuary" and "do" means "entrance"), it was an era when people felt an intimacy with water—unlike present time. The word *Inase*, which was a dashing style loved by the Edo people, was also associated with the vigor of waves.

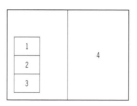

1 Fine pattern of waves - 1
● CD 05_147 ● Navy blue
This is a good example that shows how rough waves can even be expressed even by small dots.

2 Fine pattern of waves - 2
● CD 05_148 ● blue-green
The waves shown in this pattern are far calmer than in example number 147. This impression is even stronger when it is used as a continuous pattern.

3 Fine pattern of waves - 3
● CD 05_149 ● dark blue
The impression given by the whirling waves in this pattern could be considered as too overpowering when used in a kimono design.

4 Waves on firemen's costumes
● CD 05_150 ● violet blue
This rough wave pattern, that was used on firefighters' costumes is one example of Edo style. Naturally, water always opposes fire.

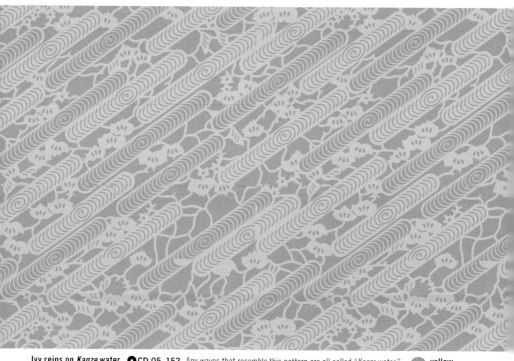

***Seigai* waves** ●CD 05_151 The white design of the *Seigai* waves in a fine pattern. Despite the fact that much of this pattern has changed, it still retains its original appearance.

sky blue

Ivy reins on *Kanze* water ●CD 05_152 Any waves that resemble this pattern are all called "*Kanze* water." It is an elegant flowing water pattern with distinguishing features.

yellow and pink

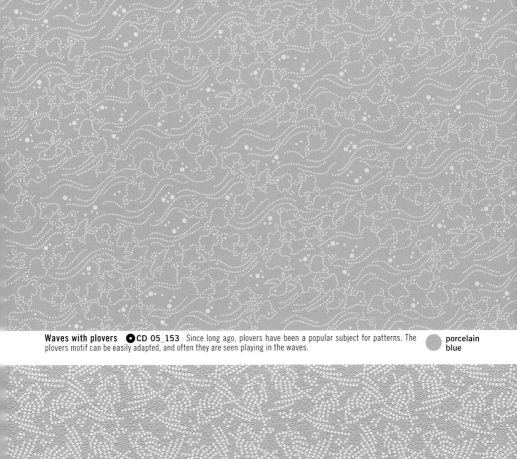

Waves with plovers ●CD 05_153 Since long ago, plovers have been a popular subject for patterns. The plovers motif can be easily adapted, and often they are seen playing in the waves.

 porcelain blue

Floating rafts (delivering logs by a flowing river) ●CD 05_154 Indirectly, this pattern conveys the feel of water and a peaceful effect.

fawn

● CD 05 155 – 158
Chiyogami
(Paper with colorful patterns)

The tastes of the Edo people are clearly reflected in the *"Edo Chiyogami"*

Apparently *Chiyogami* (paper with colorful patterns) became popular among women during Edo times. The origin was *Fuki-e* (the technique of making a painting by spraying paint over a cut-out pattern) and was used in Edo culture in *Nishiki-e* (colored woodcuts) shops by *Ukiyoe* (woodblock print) artists to make cheap paper prints. In this way, Edo *Chiyogami* paper clearly reflects the tastes of the Edo people.

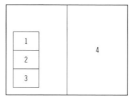

1 *Chiyogami* **wave pattern** ● royal blue
● CD 05_155

The designer of this pattern is unknown, but it looks like part of the pattern of a *Kohrin* wave. The special feature of this pattern is the way the direction of the wave changes. It needs a little work done on it, however, to make it into a continuous pattern.

2 *Chiyogami* **water pattern** ● spruce green
● CD 05_156

This is a blend of several different water patterns. It is a popular *Chiyogami* wave pattern because it can be expanded without limits.

3 **Waves on dyed futon cloth** ● indigo
● CD 05_157

These are waved dyed on futon material. The waves are brought to life with vigorous brush strokes.

4 **Pattern-dyed waves** ● seaweed-green
● CD 05_158 ● sea-blue

This represents the raging sea. By moving the pattern, it is possible to increase the intensity of the waves. This pattern conveys the fear that must have been felt by the large junk ships in such violent waters.

● CD 05 159 – 162
Vivid Depictions

A cultivated sense is reflected in both literature and patterns

Literature is one part of Edo culture that has an elevated reputation. The way of thinking and habits that are vividly described in popular stories and inexpensive, illustrated storybooks—in Haiku and Senryu— richly influenced the lifestyle of the Edo people. Patterns share a common background; they are created by the observing humans and nature, and have their roots in the atmosphere of the times, which cultivated the sense of expression. It is the same close relationship as the intimate connection that developed between Japanese songs and patterns.

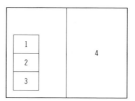

1 Snow pellets　　　　　　　　　　● China blue
● CD 05_159

The way that the designer of this pattern chose to express snow in crescent shapes rather than round shapes conveys an understanding of how the echoing of a slow Japanese drum beat during a play can create a sense of the cold.

2 Different-sizes of snow　　　　　● light gray-green
● CD 05_160

The origin of this design is from a *kamishimo* (an Edo-period ceremonial dress of the warrior class.) This is a restrained and noble pattern.

3 *Seigai* waves welling up　　　　● subdued pink
● CD 05_161

This is a perfect expression of rising movement and the world of Haiku.

4 Mist and water drops pattern　　● mid-lilac
● CD 05_162

This pattern expresses the sentiment in ● cherry-blossom pink
the *Senryu* poem titled, "Spring Mist Next to the Edo Cherry Blossoms." *Sakuradamon* was the name of one entrance to the Edo castle and *Kasumi* was the shortened name for *Kasumigaseki* – an area that the words of the *Senryu* tell us had so many buildings in it that there was hardly enough space left to live in.

Clouds ●CD 05_163 Because each unit takes on a diamond shape, this pattern could also be called "cloud diamonds." **dark indigo blue**

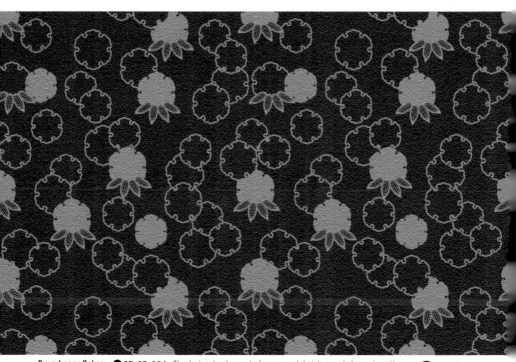

Round snowflakes ●CD 05_164 The design development of snow crystals into round shapes in patterns was seen from the Momoyama period. I ● **purple-navy blue**

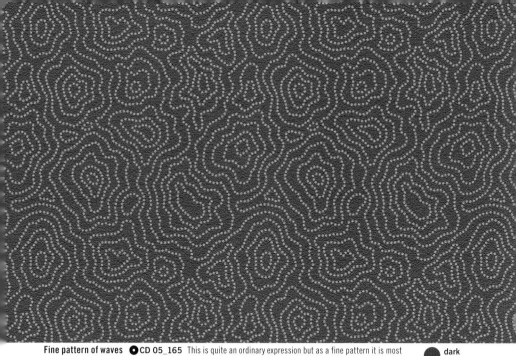

Fine pattern of waves ●CD 05_165 This is quite an ordinary expression but as a fine pattern it is most appropriate.

dark green

Running ink ●CD 05_166 As seen in pattern number 165, just by changing the dimensions of the dots gives a wide variety of different expressions.

 black ink

● CD 05 167 – 170
Developing Designs

Outstanding development of symbols inspired by a deep reverence for nature

It may be easy to develop symbols (and designs) from plants and animals. However, it is an extremely difficult skill to take any natural phenomenon that does not have a fixed shape, develop it into a symbol and pattern and, at the same time, capture its inherent qualities. The excellent design skills of symbolizing natural phenomena, as shown in the design of family crests, are rarely seen outside of Japan. This is not just because Japanese people are ethnically homogeneous; it is also a result of the deep reverence felt by the Japanese people towards nature.

1		4
2		
3		

1 Welling up　　　　　　　　　　　light gray
● CD 05_167
This is the original form of a "welling-up" pattern. By inserting different motifs between the curved lines, this pattern was given the name "motifs welling-up."

2 Bamboo welling up in *Yorokejima* 　light blue
(cloth woven in a striped pattern)
CD 05-168 (light blue)
● CD 05_168
The welling-up striped pattern appears woven and has become a fixed form.

3 Lightning pattern　　　　　　　　light lilac
● CD 05_169
The original form of this pattern comes from China. This fine pattern has been developed by adapting the original form, just a little, to remove the exotic feel of it.

4 Flowers, birds, wind and moon　　cherry
● CD 05_170　　　　　　　　　　blossom pink
The Japanese lettering for the words "flowers, birds, wind, and moon" have been incorporated into this pattern.

● CD 05 171 – 174

Scenery

The tastes of the Edo people continue even now

The creation of symbols for scenery entailed many painstaking techniques. However, our ancestors tackled the task and were successful. They went much further than vague expressions of scenery: the sky was blue, the forest was green, the mist was light and, the foot of the mountain was faraway. The artisans even produced patterns that seemed to lock in the sound of a birdsong. What was developed by the Edo people is still being carried on today.

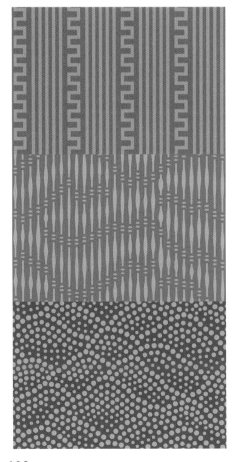

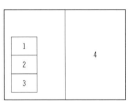

1 Flat mountain path and stripes — brown
● CD 05_171
We cannot call this a jagged pattern. The pattern's name has been established as "flat mountain path and stripes."

2 Variation on a mountain path — grass green
● CD 05_172
This impressive pattern easily conjures up the image of a lush mountain path.

3 Family crest of distant mountains — purple
● CD 05_173
This is a well-known pattern depicting mist hanging over the mountains. It creates a peaceful atmosphere and is not at all heavy.

4 Variation on a peonies and mountain path pattern — dark gray / bright pink
● CD 05_174
The steep mountains create a 3D effect in the stripes, and the image of the peonies is projected as if you're looking through a zoom lens. The connection behind this combination of peonies and mountain path is based on the number twenty. The other name for the peony in Japanese is "twenty-day flower," and, traditionally, a journey up a steep mountain path also takes twenty days.

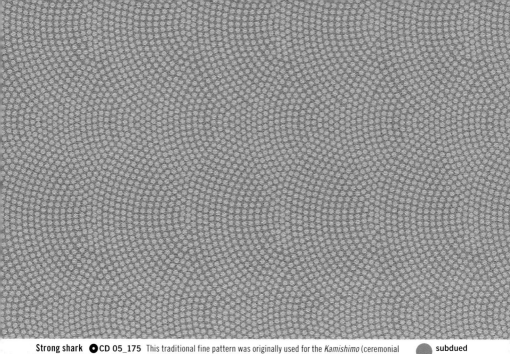

Strong shark ○CD 05_175 This traditional fine pattern was originally used for the *Kamishimo* (ceremonial kimono) of the Shimazu family from Satsuma. This is evidence of its tasteful and noble qualities.

subdued
green

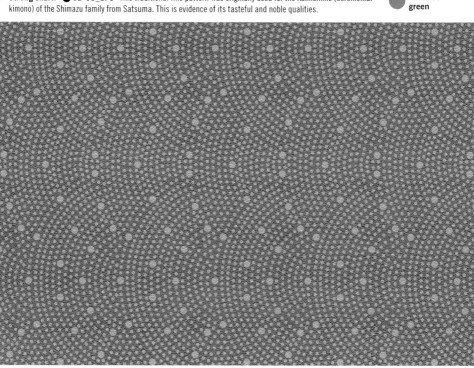

Varying dimensions in a Shimazu pattern ○CD 05_176 This is one example of many types of shark patterns.

peony
purple

Chapter 6
Geometorical Patterns
CD 06:177-250

● CD 06 177 – 180
Stylish Vertical Stripes

Examples that convey the Edo people's sense of style: subdued colors and vertical stripes

The vertical stripes pattern was first produced during "*Genrokutaihei*," which was in the Meiwa era (1751–1763) in the middle of the Edo era. At this time people were reading Ihara Saikaku's works, *Ukiyoe* (woodblock prints) became popular, and Utamaro made his debut. The Edo people had never seen the vertically striped pattern before and it became the most fashionable design of the time. Colorful patterns had become acceptable at this time and the purple preferred by the Edo people had more blue in it than red, whereas the purple from Kyoto had more red in it than blue. Edo people thought of the blue-tinged purple as reminiscent of sunset, and it also was fitting to the popularity of conservative, subdued colors in Edo society.

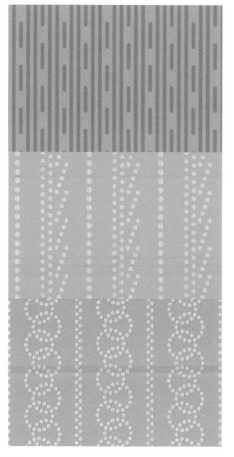

1	4
2	
3	

■ Patterns between stripes
● CD 06_177
● light brown

In contrast to woven patterns, vertical stripes were extremely popular for striped fine patterns that could be freely dyed.

■ Variations on the striped theme
● CD 06_178
● light green

A wide variety of striped woven patterns were made by varying the level of thickness or detail, color, and the space between the stripes. Fine patterns offered an endless range of variations on the striped theme.

■ Hoops and stripes
● CD 06_179
● apricot

By using different motifs in the vertical striped patterns the Edo artisans produced a diverse range of patterns.

■ Wisteria stripes
● CD 06_180
● wisteria

One can imagine how thrilled an artist would have been to see flowers used in a vertical striped pattern in such a stylish way.

Striped variation with *Sawarabi* (fresh bracken sprouts) ●CD 06_181 In this light and airy pattern a seasonal feel is conveyed by the young, fresh sprouts.

light green

Striped pattern variation ●CD 06_182 You can almost see the triumphant faces of the artisans when they produced this complicated pattern of vertical stripes that would be more or less impossible to weave.

● **dark pink**

⦿ CD 06 183 – 186
Fish Scales

Fine-pattern fish scale designs that soften the strength of the angular shape

The fish scale patterns are not as stylish as the vertical stripes patterns. One reason for this is that that the angular shape of the triangle is too sharp. Also, triangular shapes have the feel of primitive religions, and are associated with reptile scales. Although the powerful fish scale pattern was not really suitable for female clothing, it was used in Noh costumes since olden times and for *Happi* coats during the Edo era. The dyed fine patterns show evidence of the efforts made to soften the strength of the sharp point.

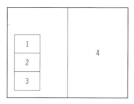

1 Fish scales
⦿ CD 06_183

● bright green

The area of background has been increased by making the triangular shapes small and separate.

2 Big and small scaled pattern
⦿ CD 06_184

● Prussian blue

This is an attractive pattern that shows creativity in reducing the overbearing quality of the angular shapes.

3 Fish scale pattern
⦿ CD 06_185

● light brown

Special skill is shown in the way the scales seem to vaguely float upwards in this pattern.

4 Fish scales with patterns inside
⦿ CD 06_186

This design conveys more of a religious image than that of a fish scale pattern.

● CD 06 187 – 190

Saya (Key or Greek fret) Shapes

Saya patterns that convey a religious effect and were used as original decorative designs

The *manji* shape was used as a symbol for sun worship during the Senshi era and was passed on to later generations as a strongly religious symbol. However, when the *saya* woven patterns first arrived in Japan from overseas the *manji* was used as a crest. They probably noticed how the *manji* formed a *saya* pattern when connected and this weakened the religious effect. This was one of the first patterns used in Japan for decorative designs.

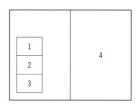

1 *Manji* and *Ayasugi* (Japanese Cedar) ● purple
● CD 06_187
This Japanese cedar bark pattern is woven like a fishing net and is used in fence patterns, among other applications.

2 Variation on the Japanese Cedar pattern ● dark green
● CD 06_188
This is a pattern developed from connecting shapes. It must present quite an interesting challenge to develop designs based on a rotating shape.

3 Flowers in Japanese Cedar ● maroon
● CD 06_189
This pattern is created by taking the motif of the Japanese cedar and bringing out a woven effect through dyeing.

4 Saya shape ● dark blue
● CD 06_190
This pattern is close to perfect. Its wonderful design demonstrates a high level of decorative design skill and the use of only indigo blue is impressive.

CD 06 191 – 194
Cloisonné

Beautiful designs (cloisonné) created by the nature of the shapes

The name for cloisonné in Japanese ("seven treasures") originates from the sound of the kanji characters for "in four directions" which is the way the circled pattern connects and continues in this design. The cloisonné treasures are: gold, silver, pearls, agate, crystal, coral and lapis lazuli. It is only natural that this design should possess auspicious qualities. But even if we ignore the attractiveness of the auspicious aspect, the naturally created design is beautiful and mesmerizing for the onlooker.

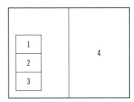

1 Cloisonné pattern - 1 — light creamy green
CD 06_191

The skillful way this pattern has been designed could only be done by a Japanese artisan. The connections to the four corners have been taken away and a paper pattern making technique has been applied.

2 Cloisonné pattern - 2 — lavender
CD 06_192

The "seven treasures symbols" can also help to develop the strong points of fine patterns.

3 Cloisonné pattern - 3 — sky blue
CD 06_193

This is a tastefully themed pattern.

4 Gold brocade, a fine cloisonné pattern — dark apricot
CD 06_194

This is a luxurious cloisonné pattern. It demonstrates the techniques of how to develop thematic patterns ranging from light to heavy.

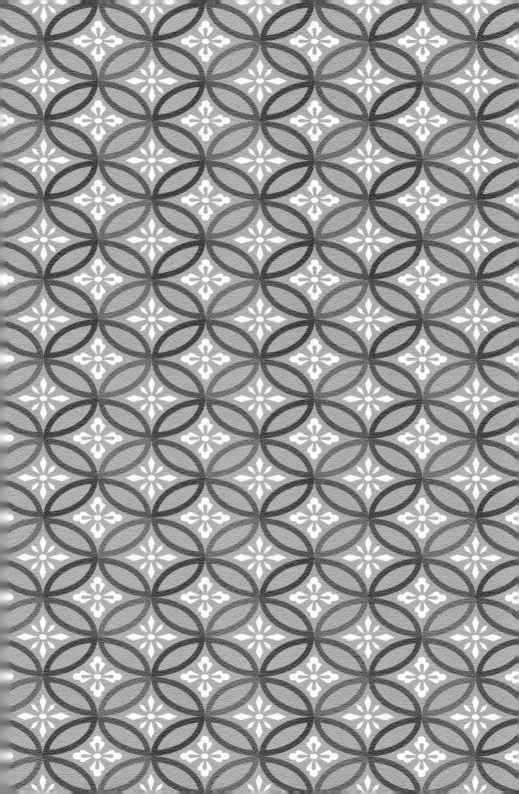

● CD 06 195 – 198

Ichimatsu (Checked patterns)

Fashion trend towards excellent and simple patterns that have universal appeal

Fashions trend toward excellent simple patterns that have universal appeal. The name of this pattern in Japanese includes the kanji character for "pine," yet there is no pine pattern in this design. This popular design was actually a representation for pine. The Edo era Kabuki actor, Sanokawa Ichimatsu, wore this design on stage in a *hakama* and it became so popular that women even started wearing the design in narrow-sleeved kimonos. This is the simple reason why it got the name "*Ichimatsu* pattern." Not all of the patterns that came into fashion had a universal appeal like this one.

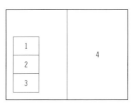

1 *Ichimatsu* check   ● Navy blue
● CD 06_195
It is only natural for such a fine pattern to be developed as an expression of an *Ichimatsu* pattern.

2 *Ichimatsu* flower diamond pattern   ● dark green
● CD 06_196
An unlimited number of variations can be developed from outstanding, yet simple, designs.

3 Patterns in *Ishidatami* (stone floor)   ● dark green
● CD 06_197
The *Ichimatsu* pattern is also known as *Ishidatami* pattern. Both names express a similar kind of sense.

4 *Ishidatami* variation   ● dark green
● CD 06_198
The name *Ichimatsu* is more suitable for this pattern than *Ishidatami*.

● CD 06 199 – 202

Shifts in Checks

Style created by long, thin vertical "checked stripes" illustrates the tastes of the Edo people.

For the Edo people, checked patterns were classified as unsophisticated. Compared to the square shape of traditional checked stripes, the long, thin shape of these checked stripes gave them more of an elegant feel. But Edo people were quite particular in their tastes, saying things like if curved lines were introduced into the checked stripes, the elegance would be lost. Also, this vertical checked striped pattern was popular because it was rather unusual. If everyone was wearing vertical striped checked patterns, then probably horizontal stripes would be considered more stylish. That gives us an insight into the innocence of the words used by the Edo people.

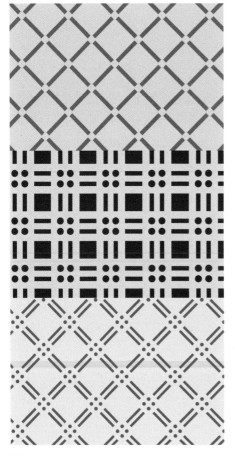

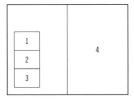

1 Single check
● CD 06_199

● light brown

This pattern demonstrates that the fine-pattern "checks" are mainly square.

2 Double check - 1
● CD 06_200

● red

The number of checked stripes increases by the use of a paper pattern to ensure that the checks do not separate.

3 Double check - 2
● CD 06_201

● blue

This pattern has the same number of stripes as in pattern number 200 but the checks have a different feel. It is more stylish than the other pattern.

4 Triple checks
● CD 06_202

● violet

This checked pattern, in which the three bars of the check are the same thickness, is called the "three-bar check" and was used by the Kabuki actor, *Danjyuro*. This pattern was very popular with boys in the Edo era.

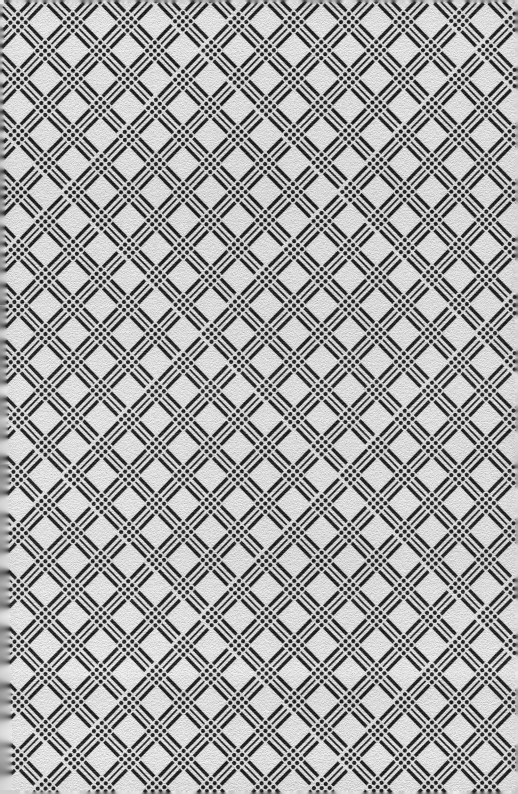

● CD 06 203 – 206

Ishidatami (Stone floor)

Ishidatami pattern inspired by the flagged stone floors of the shrines

The pattern of the stones on shrine floors is not just a simple shape; it takes on a mysterious and spiritual quality in Japan, which has many different spirits. When stones are laid on the pathways leading to the shrine, they are not stuck closely together, instead they are laid just like tatami mats, which means not only that a mere half of the number of stones is required, but also that it looks more aesthetically beautiful. The idea of using three or four squares laid together in a tatami-like fashion, rather than just one square, when designing crests, gave the designers far more scope to express their creativity in the pattern. The *Ichimatsu* pattern may well have developed from the *Ishidatami* pattern.

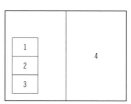

1 **Variation of *Ishidatami***
● CD 06_203

 burnt orange

This is clearly different to the *Ichimatsu* pattern. It would be impossible to develop this shape from the *Ichimatsu* pattern.

2 **Flowers in *Ishidatami***
● CD 06_204

light Prussian blue

The small flowers in this pattern transform this *Ishidatami* pattern into a pretty fine pattern.

3 **Chinese flowers in *Ishidatami***
● CD 06_205

scarlet

This pattern gives much more of a dynamic effect than pattern number 204. However, because the contrast between the colors is rather weak, it probably looks rather flat when viewed from a distance.

4 ***Ishidatami* with plums and patterns**
● CD 06_206

violet

This could also be a design developed from an *Ichimatsu* pattern. It gives the appearance of being a little too over-decorative. However what is truly wonderful is the way that the half-tones of the solid parts contrast with the layout of thematic flowers without damaging the balance of the design.

⬤ CD 06 207 – 210

Steps

Patterns with strong optical effects (stepped patterns)

"Steps" are created by cutting thick stripes vertically and shifting them. The stripes produce a naturally 3D effect and create an optical illusion. In the case of Noh costumes, these large steps are used and various motifs decorate the steps creating a deceptive effect for the viewer. In the case of the fine Edo patterns, of course, patterns like the large Noh costume patterns were not used and the patterns that effectively used these stepped patterns could actually only be loosely termed as "stepped patterns."

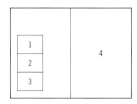

1 Variations on steps   beige
⬤ CD 06_207
This pattern is nearer to a striped rather than a stepped pattern. However, this is a modern pattern that produces visual effects like optical art.

2 Unsteady steps   tea green
⬤ CD 06_208
The steps are unsteady in this pattern. It is a rather stimulating pattern to create.

3 Variation on unsteady steps   gray-blue
⬤ CD 06_209
At a glance, this looks like a *Tachiwakubun* but with the arrangement of the squares and the shift in the pattern, the design is known as a stepped pattern.

4 Collection of fine patterns in zigzag steps   brown
⬤ CD 06_210
There are many fine patterns arranged in this pattern, all of them very tasteful.

◉ CD 06 211 – 214

Tortoiseshell

Tortoiseshell is stylish in an obi, despite the image of the name

Edo people considered geometric patterns more stylish than pictorial ones. Most of the fine patterns that developed were not connected to pictorial patterns. So it follows that fine patterns were considered stylish. The tortoiseshell pattern would probably be considered a slightly less tasteful pattern among the geometric designs. Although it is called tortoiseshell, this pattern does not give the hexagonal effect of the original shape. This wonderful tortoiseshell pattern was produced as a result of the pursuit of stylishness.

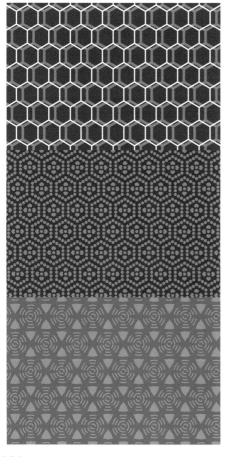

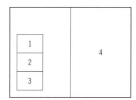

1 Tortoiseshell ● purple
◉ CD 06_211
This light and refreshing tortoiseshell pattern has an overall favorable air to it, rather than a heavy and dignified one.

2 Flowers in tortoiseshell pattern ● dark blue
◉ CD 06_212
This is a neat fine pattern that does not resemble tortoiseshell.

3 Twisted pattern ● green
◉ CD 06_213
The connecting pattern of the tortoiseshell has shifted here, and the twisted pattern is the main focus.

4 Tortoiseshell obi ● crimson
◉ CD 06_214
This pattern is often developed by combining lines, dots and smaller patterns.

● CD 06 215 – 218

Yoroke (Striped woven patterns)

The feeling of freedom is conveyed by the sophisticated curved lines generic to *yoroke*.

The *yoroke* pattern was almost unknown before the Edo period. The Edo artisans modified the shape and changed the name of the patterns and as a result it may have been the creative skills of the Edo artisans that led to the extreme popularity of *yoroke* designs in fine patterns. Just the term "curved stripes" gives a rather broad, uniform impression and does not convey the feel of freedom or sophistication in the curved lines that is seen in the *yoroke* stripes. The exactly fitting descriptions for the *yoroke* patterns may be more like "winding curved lines" or "soft and pliable curved lines."

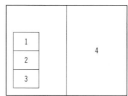

1 A variation on a *yoroke* checked pattern — light green
● CD 06_215

Skill has been applied in this pattern to create a pleasant expression. The way the stripes are lined up in a uniform way gives the pattern rhythm.

2 *Yoroke* stripes with patterns — gray
● CD 06_216

These stripes show the irrefutable meandering shape of a *yoroke* design. The inserted patterns resemble the footprints of plovers. However, the sophisticated tastes of the Edo artisans would not enable them to name this pattern "plover footprints."

3 *Yoroke* Reins — gray cherry blossom
● CD 06_217

This pattern can give the appearance of a hanging mist depending on the way you look at it, either by its color or the way the color is handled.

4 Variation on the *yoroke* theme beige
● CD 06_218

When a striped pattern that is already stylish is made into a *yoroke* pattern it becomes even more stylish.

● CD 06 219 – 222

Imported Patterns

The limited conditions in which *Shokko* patterns could be used are dictated by their over-dignified atmosphere

The *Shokko* pattern was imported from China during the Muromachi period and is known as the "*Shokko* decorative pattern." *Shokko* came from the period from around the third century in China. Hexagonal shapes are connected together and there is a secondary pattern of either diamonds or squares. There are many different kinds of patterns packed into the hexagonal shape and secondary square shape. As this pattern is dignified and has a high class feel to it, there are limitations to its usage. Even as a fine pattern it has a dignified air to it.

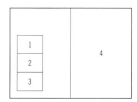

1	4
2	
3	

1 Large pattern from Korea ● wine red
● CD 06_219
This pattern is used for belts and tatami-mat edging and is a luxurious pattern originating from Korea.

2 *Shokko* pattern - 1 ● purple
● CD 06_220
At a glance this looks like a complicated pattern, but the strength of this pattern has been softened.

3 *Shokko* pattern - 2 ● dove-wing purple
● CD 06_221
This is an average-sized pattern rather than a fine pattern. When finished in one simple color it would give a high-class effect and reduce the overbearing quality.

4 Rain dragon in *Shokko* pattern ● charcoal
● CD 06_222
You can see the effort taken to produce a decorative *Shokko* pattern in the fine pattern. It shows a fighting spirit.

● CD 06 223 – 226
Double Patterns

Designs expressed by two patterns

Spectacular strides were made in color dying during the Edo era. The transition from woven to dyed patterns was a natural path leading toward mass production and decorative design. Woodblock print designs were accurately produced by using ten pieces of wood for each part of the picture, and this was a special skill in which Japanese artisans excelled. In the case of paper pattern reproduction, the artisans found it convenient to use two sheets of paper patterns for accurately reproducing designs that could not be made by just one sheet. "Double patterns" means the use of two patterns glued together to produce a design.

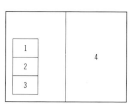

1 Double patterns - 1
● CD 06_223
● fresh green
Although this is a simple design, the dyed pattern would be impossible to produce without using two pattern sheets.

2 Double patterns - 2
● CD 06_224
● purple
This design would be possible to produce by using just one pattern if you wait for the glue to dry.

3 Tie-dyed pattern
● CD 06_225
● deep red
The double-pattern technique is necessary to create this design where both the background and main pattern are tie-dyed.

4 Chinese flowers on *yoroke* stripes
● CD 06_226
● Prussian blue
With skillful cutting and dividing this design could be created by using only one pattern, but to give the background a woven feel and to create a 3D effect two patterns are necessary.

● CD 06 227 – 230

Units Arranged in Lines

Designs with features enabling increased production in a shorter time

The most representative fine patterns are those created by using small dots to convey various expressions. However, in order to match the strong appetite of the Edo people, new patterns and designs that could be produced in a short time-scale were in demand. There is no better example of sustained efforts being made to bring about satisfactory results than that of the Edo craftsmen.

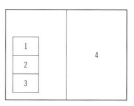

1 Variation on a checked pattern - 1   light yellow
● CD 06_227
Although the patterns themselves are nothing special, the contrast produced when they are arranged in lines in this way establishes a form in itself.

2 Variation on a checked pattern - 2   light pink
● CD 06_228
The technique used in this pattern gives a visual impression of something concrete in this abstract pattern. In this case, the back view of a woman's (peach-shaped) hairstyle.

3 Variation on a checked pattern - 3   light green
● CD 06_229
This striped pattern presents an arrangement of elliptic shapes and shadow. It looks like an arrangement of paper dolls.

1 A design using circular shapes   beige
● CD 06_230
Two kinds of pattern are randomly arranged producing a pattern that may appeal to children in particular.

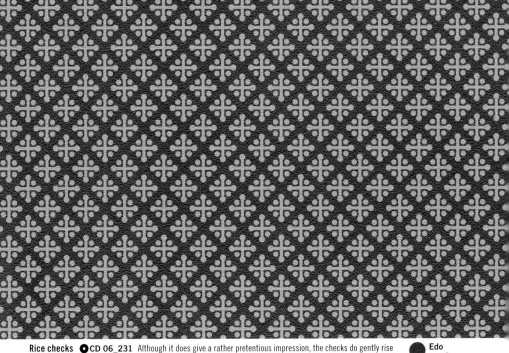

Rice checks ●CD 06_231 Although it does give a rather pretentious impression, the checks do gently rise to the surface.

 Edo purple

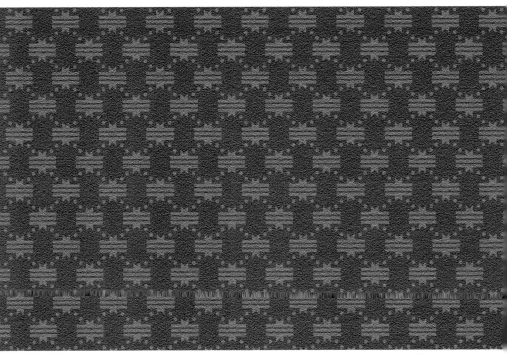

Variation on the rice motif ●CD 06_232 When the same rice pattern is used to form the shape of a spool it gives a rather more intimate impression than the one in pattern number 231.

 Edo purple

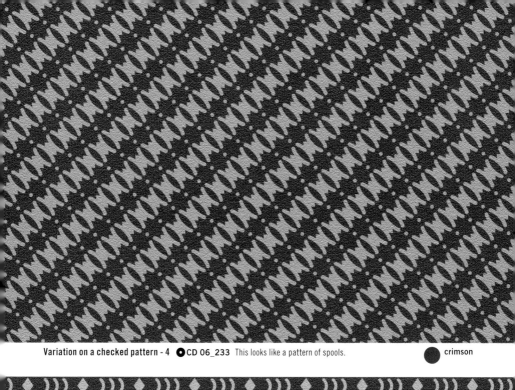

Variation on a checked pattern - 4 ● CD 06_233 This looks like a pattern of spools.　　crimson

Variation on a checked pattern - 5 ● CD 06_234 This pattern produces a rather strange effect and is a neat arrangement. However, it does not have an awkward feel to it.　　crimson

Lucky diamonds ●CD 06_235 This pattern is different to the established diamond pattern. It is simple, but not cheap-looking and has a special appeal.

spruce
green

Checks with patterns ●CD 06_236 It is possible to see many different patterns in this design, which makes it very attractive. It makes you want to know more about how it was created.

spruce
green

Variation on a diamond pattern ●CD 06_237 This pattern is beautiful in its simplicity.

dark blue

Variations on a clover pattern ●CD 06_238 The pattern unit seems to move back and forth creating an attractive contrasting 3D effect in this design.

dark blue

● CD 06 239 – 242

Diamond Checks

Fine patterns created both vertically and horizontally.

Although the diamond pattern has a rather flat effect, it also has a relaxed feel to it. So it follows that if the corner angles are 45 degrees then it is no longer a diamond pattern, but a pattern of squares. There are a surprisingly large number of variations of the diamond pattern. In this connection, the relaxing "connected diamond pattern" has special features; the way it is drawn and the noble impression that it creates has led to dozens of different names as a "flexible working pattern." The Edo artisans developed vertical and horizontal patterns by taking the connected diamond shapes and making them into diamond-checked patterns.

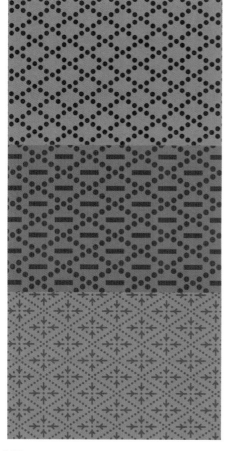

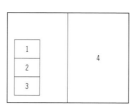

1 Diamond checks
● CD 06_239   ● light purple

Simple is best. Unmistakably, this is a diamond-checked fine pattern.

2 Bars in diamonds
● CD 06_240   ● light brown

This pattern makes you wonder why there is only one bar and not three in the diamond shapes.

3 Diamond checks with patterns insidea
● CD 06_241   ● sea blue

This pattern reinforces our understanding of how much the size of the dots influences the image of the pattern.

4 Takeda diamonds
● CD 06_242   ● subdued green

● Navy blue

This four diamond pattern is known by the name of "Takeda diamond." When the same diamond shape is used in this pattern it is called "Takeda diamond checks." Mechanical dolls wore this pattern on their clothes.

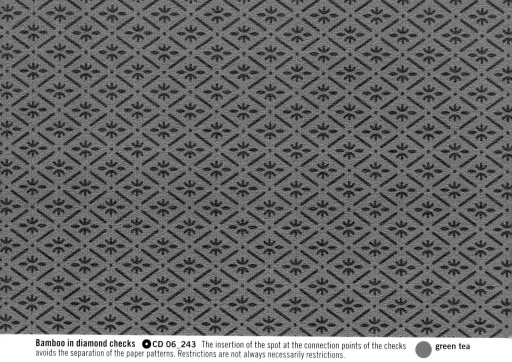

Bamboo in diamond checks ●CD 06_243 The insertion of the spot at the connection points of the checks **green tea**
avoids the separation of the paper patterns. Restrictions are not always necessarily restrictions.

Pattern in diamond checks ●CD 06_244 This is a variation on the "Diamond divided into four" pattern **green tea**
and the way small and large diamonds have been created gives it a layered effect.

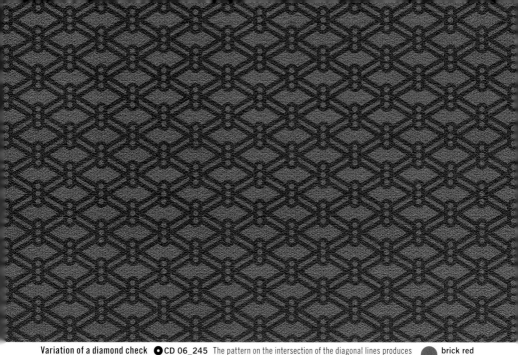

Variation of a diamond check ●CD 06_245 The pattern on the intersection of the diagonal lines produces the effect of a line crossing the pattern vertically.   ● brick red

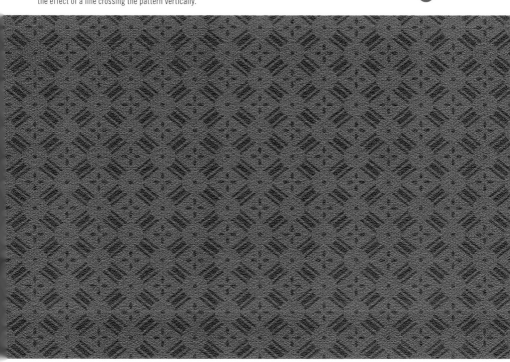

Pattern in checks ●CD 06_246 This pattern is broad but not bulky. It is a congenial pattern that conveys a sense of genius.   brick red

● CD 06 247 – 250

Variations on the Checked Patterns

Imagining the lives of the tough Edo folk.

In the Edo Kanei period (in the 1600s), some people started to sell old clothes, and after a while shops were even set up specifically for such trade. Today, they are commonly known as "second-hand shops." Not surprisingly, given the economic situation at that time, the Edo community was what we would now call "a recycling city." So it follows that many people were chasing the fashionable trends. One can imagine the powerful way the Edo people lived when looking at all of the different variations of the checked pattern.

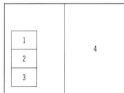

1	4
2	
3	

1 Diagonally checked pattern   ● blue
● CD 06_247
If you vary the viewing perspective, the small checks become bigger, become flowers, produce a contrast, and become diagonal checks.

2 Variation on a checked pattern   ● purple
● CD 06_248
The striped part is made smaller and shifted producing positive and negative squares. It looks like an enjoyable experimental design.

3 Checked variety   ● red
● CD 06_249
Fascinating checks have been created by the addition of "steps" inside the checks.

4 Flowing checked pattern   charcoal
● CD 06_250
This unique and original design has multiple applications.

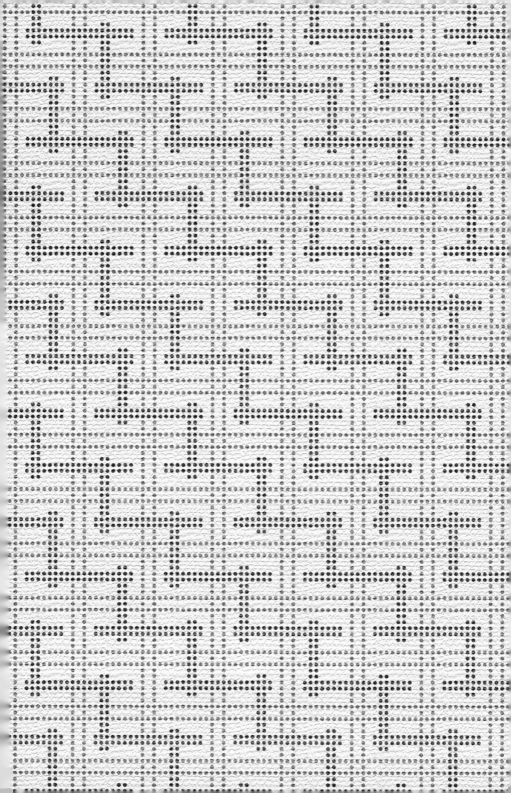

The Attached CD-ROM: Using the Material Provided

The purchaser of this book is permitted unrestricted use of the data recorded on the accompanying CD-ROM, either in its original form or in a modified fashion.

Credit or other such acknowledgment need not be noted in the event of such use. The data provided may also be used overseas, as use is not regionally restricted. Furthermore, copyright fees or secondary user fees are not required to use this material.

Adobe and Adobe Photoshop are either registered trademarks or trademarks of Adobe Systems, Incorporated registered in the United States and/or other countries. Microsoft, Windows, and Windows

XP are either registered trademarks or trademarks of Microsoft Corporation registered in the United States and other countries. Apple, Macintosh, Mac and Mac OS are either registered trademarks or trademarks of Apple Computer, Inc., registered in the United States and other countries.

All other brand and product names and registered and unregistered trademarks are the property of their respective owners.

About the Author

Shigeki Nakamura An art director since 1964, he established Cobble Collaboration Co. Ltd. in 1987. The company published a book of ESP Pattern Library Digital Materials, which can be seen on its website (cobbleart.com). He has received many awards, such as the Minister of International Trade and Industry Award, and he is a member of the JAGDA (Japanese Graphic Designer Association).